PONCE DE LEÓN

PONCE DE LEÓN AND THE DISCOVERY OF FLORIDA

The Man, the Myth, and the Truth

DOUGLAS T. PECK

ISBN 1–880654-02–4.
Library of Congress Catalogue Card No. 93–83738.

FRONT COVER DRAWING from woodcut in Antonio de Herrera y Tordesillas, *La Historia General de los Hechos de los Castellanos en las Islas y Tierra Firme.* Antwerp: Juan Bautista Verdusen, 1728.

BACK COVER PHOTOGRAPH by Chris Mikula, *The Bradenton Herald.*

Portions of "Reconstruction and Analysis of the 1513 Discovery Voyage of Juan Ponce de León" by Douglas T. Peck, contained in the October, 1992 issue of the *Florida Historical Quarterly,* have been adapted from and are reprinted with permission of the *Florida Historical Quarterly.*

Dedication

To my wife Becky.
Her vital and supportive role in keeping my family and business affairs running smoothly at home during my six and seven month long research voyages was a very real part of the total effort which produced this book.

Contents

Preface

The font the Spanish sought in vain
Through all the land of flowers
Leaps glittering from the sandy plain
Our classic grove embowers.
Here youth, unchanging blooms and smiles,
Here dwells eternal spring,
And warms from Hope's eternal isles
The winds their perfume brings.

(From "The Fountain of Youth" by Oliver Wendell Holmes, *Atlantic Monthly,* August 1873, 209–210.)

In 1873 Oliver Wendell Holmes wrote this poetical picture of Juan Ponce de León's quest for the fountain of youth. The vision lives on to this day. We must ask if the vision of Ponce de León is really true to historical fact and reality.

Juan Ponce de León is a romantically popular but little understood figure in history whose life story has all the aspects of a bed of riddles covered by a hazy blanket of myths. Ponce de León's only claim to fame seems to be that he unknowingly became the first Spanish explorer to set foot on the North American shore while searching for a fabled and mythical fountain of youth.

But there is more to the story than that, much more!

I first became interested in Ponce de León in 1988 while pursuing my research in the history of Columbus' discovery voyage, trying to pin down just which island in the Bahamas was really his first landfall in the New World. Following Columbus' navigational log, I re-sailed and reconstructed his voyage in my sailing yacht "Gooney Bird" and determined that his landfall in the Bahamas was the island of San Salvador.

I performed this reconstruction of Columbus' voyage in "Gooney Bird" by faithfully following every compass heading and distance in his log across the Atlantic from his departure point in the Canaries. I found by using this new empirical and pragmatic research method that the National Geographic Society was wrong in naming Samana Cay as the landfall island, determined initially by plotting his track across the Atlantic with a computer.

But it is very difficult to tell the National Geographic Society that it was wrong, so I needed more proof. That is what brought about my interest in Ponce de León. During his voyage to the shores of Florida, he landed on an island in the Bahamas which his Indian guides told him was "Guanahaní," Columbus' first landfall in the New World. Like Columbus, Ponce de León left a log giving compass courses, distances, descriptions of landfalls, and Indian names of islands, even latitudes, so I resolved to faithfully follow that log in "Gooney Bird," first to determine which island in the Bahamas was Guanahaní, then to locate just exactly where he landed on the shores of Florida.

I was spurred on in this endeavor after reading a footnote written by the respected historian Samuel Eliot Morison in his book *The European Discovery of America: The Southern Voyages* (1974) in which (speaking of Ponce de León's voyage) he stated, "what we now need is an historically minded yachtsman who, Herrera (i.e., Ponce de León's log) in hand, will follow Ponce's route from San Juan on the 1513 voyage, and study the shores of Florida to ascertain exactly where he called." That did it! I decided to re-trace Ponce de León's voyage in "Gooney Bird" and started gathering my research material on his 1513 voyage of discovery to include a copy of his log.

Ponce de León's log contained much more information than just the navigational data I needed to re-sail and re-trace his voyage. And it was in a comprehensive and searching study of his log and other supporting documents that I was to discover the real truth about his epic voyage which is far removed from the distorted fantasy and fiction contained in our history books and encyclopedias.

He was not the least interested in a fountain of youth, but instead was looking for a large and wealthy island called "Beniny." Nor did he land at St. Augustine, but at a point more than 125 miles south. He did not land on the Yucatan Peninsula and thus discover Mexico, but instead was carried by the Gulf Stream to the unexplored western shores of Cuba. These are but a few of the fallacies and anomalies about Ponce de León's voyage which you will find revealed in this book.

Later Ponce de León attempted to colonize the territory occupied by the Calusa Indians in South Florida. In the concluding chapter I will provide information about the Calusa and the reasons for Ponce's failed colonization efforts.

This book contains no fiction or unsupported rumors or myths which cloud previous written histories of the Ponce de León voyage. It is an outgrowth of several technical research papers I have written on the subject which have been widely accepted by the academic community both here and abroad. Material on my Ponce de León voyage, for example, appeared in my article in the October, 1992 issue of the *Florida Historical Quarterly*. While my research papers were liberally sprinkled with footnotes to substantiate and document every key or controversial statement, I have elected in this case to report my source documents in the body of the text and only then for the most important or controversial matters. But let me assure the reader that only verifiable true historical facts are within these pages.

Read on and you will find the true story of a bold and courageous conquistador, who while seeking fame and fortune in new lands was to find only disappointment and death, but who nevertheless left a legacy of discovery in the New World second only to that of Columbus.

DOUGLAS T. PECK
Bradenton, Florida
March 10, 1993.

Acknowledgments

I must acknowledge the vital role my colleagues in the Society for the History of Discoveries played in the preparation of this book. Their expertise in the discipline of historical research was unselfishly shared with me in my sometimes painful transition from an ocean navigator to research historian. Included in this group of erudite scholars are John Parker, David Buisseret, James Kelley, Oliver Dunn, David Henige, Helen Wallis, Donald McGuirk, Neil Sealey, Dan Amato, Thornton Thomas, and Robert Tolf.

Jim Kelley deserves special recognition for his scholarly translation of the original 1601 edition of Herrera's summary of Ponce de León's voyage, and the analysis of sixteenth century magnetic variation in the New World, both of which he prepared from his inexhaustible fund of historically related knowledge to support my 1990 research voyage.

My research for the book involved the use of my sailing yacht "Gooney Bird" in long and specialized voyages, the preparation for which required technical advice and assistance from many friends involved in my sailing enterprises. They are too numerous to mention but they know who they are and to them I extend my heartfelt thanks and wish them "Fair Winds."

The publishers of this book, Leo J. Harris and Moira F. Harris, are enthusiastic historians in their own right and went far beyond the normal obligations expected of a publisher by running down and furnishing me some of my bibliographic material. John and Molly in editing (and substantially improving) my manuscript were most tolerant when confronted with my seven, eight, and even nine line sentences, patiently acquainting me with the physical appearance and functioning properties of a period.

My son Douglas W. Peck also played a vital role in the production of the manuscript. My computer and word processor is definitely not user-friendly and I constantly found it would refuse to follow my instructions, even talking back to me in a derogatory manner. In this I am blessed with the fact that Douglas is a business education teacher and an expert on computers, so he was able to solve my problems quickly and easily, allowing me to complete the book within sometimes formidable deadlines.

Ponce de León, the Man and the Myth

Juan Ponce de León was born in 1474 in San Tervas del Campo, Valladolid province, in central Spain. The distinguished León family dynasty held sway over much of the Iberian peninsula in the fifteenth and sixteenth century, tracing their family lineage back to the Visigoth kings of the Roman period. The León fiefdoms were the first to join Queen Isabella in the fifteenth century in her bid to unite the Kingdom of Aragon (by marrying King Ferdinand) and then bring together the many feudal warlords in Castille under one Spanish monarchy. It was from this noble Visigothic León family heritage that Juan Ponce de León obtained his character and physique, being red-haired, robust, virile, and brave and aggressive in warfare.

Juan Ponce de León is far more famous today than he was in his own time. In the early sixteenth century his voyages and conquests lacked the epic proportions of the dazzling conquests of Cortés, Pizarro, Balboa, De Soto, or Coronado, so his exploits were overshadowed and largely forgotten or ignored by historians of the time. Ponce de León's primary achievement was to provide the basis for the settlements of Puerto Rico and Florida, which today are of major importance, but in the sixteenth century were considered of little value.

Because of the scant and contradictory information available on his early life, many historians have written that Ponce de León came from humble birth, but such is far from the truth. Prior to 1960 very little was known of Ponce de León's family until two Spanish-speaking Puerto Rican scholars, in independent research efforts, unearthed some new and valuable fifteenth and sixteenth century documents in their search of both private and public archives in Spain. The first of these was the Catholic prelate and historian Vicente Murga Sanz who, in a complicated analysis of the Ponce de León genealogy, asserts that the Florida Juan Ponce de León was one of twenty-one illegitimate children of the historically important Count Juan Ponce de León. The potent Count Juan Ponce de León sired Rodrigo Ponce de León (also illegitimate) who was the celebrated second Cid Campeador of Spain and the brother of the Florida Juan Ponce de León. The genealogy of the

Figure 1. Ponce de León near the walls of Granada.

Ponce de León lineage is filled with illegitimate offspring but, under Spanish moral standards of the day, this in no way affected their standing as accepted members of the aristocracy.

The other Puerto Rican scholar to pursue this subject was the well known and respected historian Aurelio Tío. Tío agrees with Murga Sanz on the names of many of the brothers, cousins, nephews, and uncles of the Florida Ponce de León, but names a different father, one Pedro Ponce de León.

To sort out this confusion I relied on a comprehensive analysis of these different views by Charles W. Arnade in a thoroughly documented monograph published in 1976 in *Tequesta, the Journal of the Historical Association of Southern Florida.* Arnade favors the Tío view and states that illegitimacy is responsible for this confusion which results in vast genealogical claims in all directions. He then goes on to show that the illegitimacy of Juan Ponce de León hardly mattered as it is quite apparent that he was related by blood to the celebrated Rodrigo Ponce de León, a heroic figure in the last phase of the Moorish expulsion from Spain.

Another indication that Juan Ponce de León was an aristocrat comes from the sixteenth century Spanish historian Gonzalo Fernandez de Oviedo y Valdés who reported that he served as a page to Pedro Nuñez de Guzman. Pedro Nuñez de Guzman was Grand Master of the Order of Calatrava and a confidant of the Spanish crown. To be appointed as his page would have been reserved for only young aspirant knights of the highest rank of noble blood. It is apparent that Juan Ponce de León fought in the conquest of Granada alongside his celebrated older brother Rodrigo and his mentor Pedro Nuñez de Guzman. Oviedo reports that when Juan Ponce de León arrived in the Indies he was an experienced military man having learned his trade in the war against the Moors.

Ponce de León was a product of the feudal knighthood system and was trained in warfare from an early age. There is every indication that he actively entered the war against the Moors when only fourteen years of age. Then at age eighteen, when the fighting was over in 1492, he joined the swollen ranks of Spanish unemployed knights.

In those days there were only three occupations that were considered fit for a young knight and these were going to church, going to war, and making love, and not necessarily in that order. Thus when the Spanish war against the Moors ended, the young aspiring knight and future conquistador Ponce de León had to fall back on his only remaining options for respectable employment, that of going to church or making love, and if he was anything like the Count he had no trouble with the latter. However, he apparently soon tired of this and longed for something more exciting for in 1493, when he was nineteen years old, he signed on as one of 200 gentleman volunteers on Columbus' second voyage to the newly discovered Indies.

Columbus ranged the length of the islands of the Antilles in this voyage and at one point anchored his seventeen vessels in Añasco Bay on the western shore of Puerto Rico. While at Añasco Bay, Ponce de León would have observed the beautiful Añasco valley with its fertile plain surrounded by low rounded hills covered with lush tropical growth. This might very well be what inspired him to make this area his capital when at a later date he conquered Puerto Rico and became its first governor.

Columbus' seventeen vessels were filled with soldiers, laymen from all the trades, priests, representatives of the Crown, and the gentlemen volunteers (i.e., unemployed knights) who were to colonize the island of Española (Hispaniola). In this process the first task was to subjugate the Indians and round them up as slaves to work the gold mines or the plantations. Here was a task for which the young conquistador Ponce de León was ideally suited.

Figure 2. Indians panning for gold.

Subjugation of the Indians was ruthlessly pursued for the next decade. Ponce de León so distinguished himself in conquering the large native kingdom of Higüey in the eastern end of Española (now the Dominican Republic) that he was made governor of that province and held that post until 1506. While Ponce de León killed many warriors in his battles to conquer Higüey there is no indication that he practiced the wanton, cruel and even sadistic torturing and killing of non-combatants as did the conquistadors Cortés, Pizarro, and De Soto who followed.

This enslavement of the native population amounted to genocide for the Taino Indians on Española and the other islands. The native population on Española in 1493 before the conquest has been estimated at 250,000. Fewer than 500 were reported alive in 1538 and they died out within the next few years. The responsibility for this genocide rests clearly on the heads of the slave owners working the mines and plantations rather than Columbus, Ponce de León, or any of the other explorers of this period. To blame them is like blaming the physician for the cancer.

Slavery had been an accepted way of life since biblical times. In all the ancient civilizations there were laws and codes governing the humane treatment of slaves by their owners. Not so in Española and the other islands where the slave owners treated the Indians like animals. An Indian of either sex big enough to work labored from dawn to dusk under the most intolerable conditions. Nursing mothers were put to work leaving the infants to die of starvation. Slave owners excused this treatment on the grounds that since the Indians were not Christians, they were condemned by the Church as heretics and so deserved no better treatment.

Of course it was not just the cruel treatment of the Indians that caused their deaths, but also the introduction of the European diseases of smallpox and measles against which the Indians had not built up an immunity. Although they were

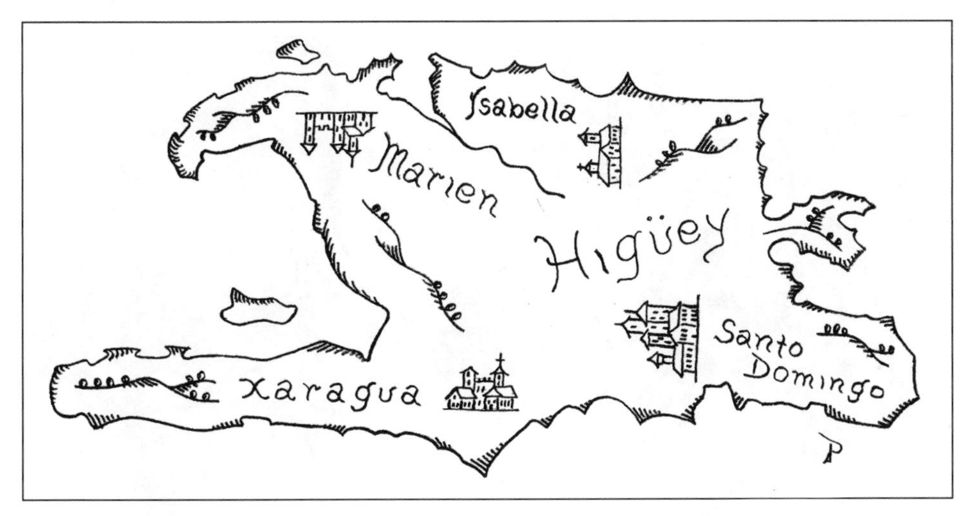

Figure 3. Map of Española.

unaware of it, the Indians can be said to have obtained their revenge on their conquerors by introducing them to syphilis and tobacco and I'm not sure which one of these is worse.

In Ponce de León's time we can see the first glimmerings of an aroused social consciousness that questioned whether the Indians should be treated as fellow human beings or enslaved. The issue was first raised by the Dominican friar Anton Montecino in a fiery sermon given in Santo Domingo, Española, in 1510. His arguments were further developed by Fray Bartolomé de Las Casas who spent a lifetime fighting for the civil rights of the Indians. Emperor Charles V finally decided that the issue had become too controversial so he sent the matter to the Council of the Indies, much as we send our social problems to the supreme court. As Lewis Hanke observed, the Emperor took the unusual step of halting all Spanish conquests until the question of slavery and the Indians had been discussed.

The Council met in Valladolid in August and September of 1550. The confrontation was between the Dominican friar Bartolomé de Las Casas, the protector of Indian rights, and Doctor Juan Gines de Sepulveda, representing the colonists who depended on slaves to stay in business. Sepulveda supported his argument for slavery by using Aristotle's remark that, "some men are by nature slaves." Sepulveda then went on to summarize his argument for slavery by saying, "just as children are inferior to adults, women to men, and monkeys to human beings, so Indians are naturally inferior to Spaniards." What a male chauvinist! But the fact of the matter is he was applauded by most of the people running the show so slavery held on for another 300 years in the New World.

With the Kingdom of Higüey thoroughly subdued and quiet, the job of governor reverted to dull routine bureaucratic administration which just didn't fit Ponce de León's restless and vigorous nature. So in 1506 he applied for permission

Figure 4. Indians smoking tobacco.

to conquer and subdue the large island of Borinquen (now Puerto Rico). Now this was more like it! Ponce de León was back in the exciting role of a conquistador and could get away from that desk and paperwork. With 100 carefully picked soldiers he set sail for Puerto Rico.

At this time the western half of Puerto Rico was occupied by the Taino Indians, the same tribe that occupied all of Española, while the cannibal tribes of Caribs occupied the eastern sector. Ponce de León made his initial landing on the western shore at Añasco Bay and prepared for battle. But the battle never came because the local Taino cacique (king) Aguaybana gave up without a fight and submitted to Spanish rule. He no doubt had heard of the invincibility of the Spanish troops and decided that discretion was the better part of valor.

Ponce de León was not to find all the Indians this subservient and it took him several years to subdue the entire island. The principal trouble makers were the bellicose and warlike Caribs entrenched on the eastern end of the island.

The cannibalistic Carib tribes began their migration northward through the islands of the Antilles from the northern shores of South America about 1000 A.D. They followed a similar migration of the Arawak speaking Taino Indians who had

Figure 5. The islands of the cannibals.

moved north through the islands about the time of Christ and displaced the primitive hunter-gatherer Ciboney Indians. In the early sixteenth century, the few remaining Ciboney Indians were barely hanging on in the hills of western Cuba and the first Caribs were those whom Ponce de León encountered on the eastern shores of Puerto Rico.

The fierce and pugnacious nature of the Caribs was perhaps due to their high protein diet and they had a number of unsavory and repugnant methods for maintaining that diet. According to several early commentators they ate only the captured male members of other tribes, saving the female captives to breed more males whom they would castrate and fatten for the dinner table in pens, much as we do in our cattle industry. The cultural tradition of killing and eating only the males is common to many other cannibal cultures around the world and has its origins in a distant religious cult doctrine of eating captured male warriors to infuse their bravery and strength into the body of the captor.

Taino Indians told Columbus about an island named Matinino (probably St. Croix) a short distance east of Carib (definitely Puerto Rico). This island was inhabited only by women who were visited by the Caribs once each year. The women retained their female children and sent away the males. Columbus and naive historians of the sixteenth century were to picture this island as the home of Amazon warriors as in the Greek myths, when in reality it was just a cattle ranch for the Caribs. Anthropologists tell us that if the Spaniards had not killed off the gentle and passive Taino Indians when they did, the Caribs would have done the job within the next 500 years as they migrated north through the islands.

Some recent scholars (most recently, Philip Boucher in his book *Cannibal Encounters*) writing on the subject of the Carib Indians infer that the Spanish explorers and conquistadors exaggerated or embellished the accounts of Carib cannibalism to justify their killing of the Caribs and the take over of their lands. They cite the reports of certain missionaries (usually French) who lived among the few remaining Caribs in the islands of the lesser Antilles long after the Spanish era, and conclude that there is very little documentary proof for anthropophagy ("cannibalism," derived from Carib or canibali, replaced anthropophagy as a term in popular speech for man-eating in the fifteenth century) in the islands. There probably is some basis of truth in the Spaniards' exaggeration of the amount or degree of cannibalism among the Caribs. However, in weighing the Spaniards' first encounter testimony from many sources against the testimony of others who appeared on the scene after the Carib culture had virtually been wiped out, I would manifestly give more weight to the Spaniards' initial report of cannibalism than to the later "arguments from silence" for which very little documentary proof can be found.

There was no record of a Carib Indian ever submitting to slavery so the Crown set out on a program of extermination and offered a bounty of land grants to conquistadors based upon the number of Caribs killed. Lest we lose sight of the reason or justification for this killing, we must remember that the Inquisition during this period was torturing and putting to death Europeans for far lesser crimes than the heresy of cannibalism. Ponce de León was to benefit from this program and at a later date would move his Carib hunters from Puerto Rico to St. John and other nearby islands.

Ponce de León, like other conquistadors, used large hunting dogs to round up Indians for slaves, or in warfare to attack and kill or disable an enemy on command. This use of dogs is not unlike our present use of attack dogs by many metropolitan police forces. The sixteenth century Spanish historian Oviedo reported that Ponce de León had a rather famous greyhound named Becerillo who could distinguish by smell a friend from an enemy Indian and in battle was worth fifty men. Oviedo described Becerillo as "of red pelt and black eyes, medium sized and not bad looking." The Caribs got him in the end, but not before he had sired a pup which Balboa took with him in the conquest of Panama.

Following the military campaign to conquer Puerto Rico, Ponce de León was confirmed by the Crown as governor of the island in 1509. He established his government at San German, a short distance up the Añasco river from his initial landing site. Without a doubt Ponce de León would have acquired large land grants in this area and we will see later that he was to return here at the start of his voyage in 1513 to provision his ships from his plantations. As reported earlier, Ponce de León probably obtained a good view of this landing site when he was aboard one of Columbus' seventeen vessels which were anchored here in November, 1493. From all reports Ponce de León served three years as governor with exceptional skill, bringing peace and prosperity to the island, but his tenure in office was cut short by politics of the time.

Ponce de León was relieved without prejudice as governor of Puerto Rico when Diego Colón (Columbus' eldest son) asserted the right to appoint governors of the islands as was clearly spelled out in his father's contract with the Sovereigns. This set the stage for the next great adventure of Ponce de León when he discovered and named "La Florida." Actually, Ponce de León was probably glad to be relieved of the dull and tedious job as governor which would free him for more exciting adventures and conquests. And what greater adventure could there be than seeking and conquering a new island?

Although already an extremely wealthy aristocrat on good terms with the Sovereigns, Ponce de León had this insatiable urge of the Spanish conquistador to obtain more wealth and prestige. So at this time, as "he had news that they found lands to the north," Ponce de León naturally resolved to find and conquer this new land. As required by the law of the times he applied to King Ferdinand for permission to seek and conquer "Beniny" where he would be the Adelantado (governor) and reap benefits in honor and wealth.

Permission to explore was closely controlled by the Crown in the form of an official charter or patent and was not issued open ended. Rather, this document covered all aspects of the destination and mission. He was issued an official patent in February, 1512 which spelled out in detail his authority and mission. An examination of this patent reveals that Ponce de León was authorized to seek and claim the "island of Beniny." *There is no mention of a fountain of youth,* but a detailed accounting procedure was given for the immense wealth that Indian rumor and folklore attributed to Beniny and its surrounding islands.

Where did Ponce de León get his information about "lands to the north" and about the wealthy "island of Beniny"? And just what was he really looking for? The answer to these questions and the navigational data I needed to accurately re-sail and re-trace Ponce de León's voyage were acquired by an in-depth study of all available original source documents pertaining to the voyage.

The only extant source giving details of Ponce de León's voyage which includes navigational data is Antonio de Herrera's *Historia General de los hechos de los Castellanos en las Islas i tierra firme del Mar Oceano,* which was published between 1601 and 1615. Herrera was appointed to the position as Spain's official Historiographer of the Indies by Phillip II in 1592. This position would have given Herrera access to the official and secret archives and to Ponce de León's original holograph log or to a copy since destroyed.

In my research I used three English translations of Herrera's chapter on Ponce de León's voyage. Florence P. Spofford's translation was contained in the monograph on Ponce de León by T. Frederick Davis, published by the Florida Historical Society in 1935. L. D. Scisco's translation was published by the American Geographical Society in 1913. The latest and best was a recently published translation by James E. Kelley, Jr., in the *Revista de Historia de America*. This work, which carries the English translation adjacent to the Spanish text, is from the original 1601 publication and contains copious footnotes explaining possible differences in interpretation of sixteenth century words.

Some scholars question the validity of using the navigational data in Herrera's account because it is a summary rather than a direct copy of the original holograph log. Herrera summarized and abridged Ponce de León's log in the same manner that Las Casas summarized and abridged Columbus' log. Both were done from the original holograph document or a scribe's copy. Unfortunately, Herrera added numerous comments that were based on knowledge obtained after 1513, and were not contained in the original log. This has led some scholars to believe that Herrera authored the entire account and that the navigational data are his and not extracted from the original log. These additions by Herrera are easily identified, however, and when they are removed, the original log entries of compass headings, times, distances, descriptions of landfalls, latitudes, identification of known islands with Indian names, sea conditions, and weather (all of which are elements of a navigator's log) come through with clarity. Why should they lose their value just because they come to us summarized by a second person?

But what of the accuracy of the data contained in Ponce de León's log? Here there are several stumbling blocks. The latitudes for the islands and certain shore features do not agree with known facts. His compass courses would seem to put him ashore in some places, and in others he would have been far at sea when he reported land. There are viable answers to these questions which are revealed in the reconstruction of the voyage following. But first we must examine the purpose and goal of the voyage as spelled out in his official patent from the Crown to determine where he intended to sail and just what he expected to find.

The official patent issued by the Crown and containing details of the mission and destination of the voyage, is found in *Coleccion de Documentos Ineditos del Archivo de Indias*. As translated by Dr. J. A. Robertson, it appears in T. Frederick Davis' 1935 article for the Florida Historical Society. The remaining source documents which I used in my research and analysis of the voyage, are noted in the text or contained in the bibliography.

In my study and analysis of these documents, I discovered two glaring examples which show how our history books and encyclopedias are wrong in their reporting of facts concerning the Ponce de León voyage.

The first error is in determining Ponce de León's age at the time of his voyage. Most history and reference books state that Ponce de León was born in 1460 and that is wrong by a good fourteen years. At an inquest in Seville on 28 September 1514, following his discovery voyage, he swore on oath that he was 40 years old (stating one's age was required at all inquests). A copy of the record of this inquest is still in the Archives of the Indies in Seville.

My earlier report of the birth date of Ponce de León as 1474 is the correct date and this would make him a strapping, healthy and vigorous 39 year old conquistador at the time of his voyage, hardly in need of a fountain of youth.

So that brings us to the second error in our history books which is that Ponce de León was looking for a fountain of youth in his 1513 exploration voyage. I will later show why we should put to bed this apocryphal story that Ponce de León was looking for a fountain of youth when he discovered Florida. But first let's examine where this fountain of youth myth came from and how it was injected (wrongfully) into our history books as the purpose of Ponce de León's voyage.

The fountain of youth is a myth which can be found in various forms in the folklore of most ethnic cultures in Europe and the Middle East. It was associated with the Prester John myth of Ethiopia and Alexander the Great is alleged to have found a spring whose waters restored his aging warriors. Alexander the Great's tie to the fountain of youth could be of Arabic origin. In the long Arabian story dealing with Alexander he searched in the Land of Darkness for the Well of Life to prolong his allotted lifespan. Health-giving spas and medicinal warm mineral baths were a part of everyday life in the sixteenth century, but the "miraculous" powers of the mythical fountain far exceeded those of such known waters. This myth, together with other Eurasian myths such as the Amazon warriors and the seven cities of Cibola, were simply transplanted to the New World as romantic fiction by historians and writers of the early sixteenth century.

The fountain of youth appears in different accounts as a fountain, river, spring, or as miraculous and rejuvenating waters, but they are all talking about the same thing. The fountain is associated with sensual, erotic love and either drinking or bathing in the waters could restore youthful sexual performance lost with age. And this is a powerful force for keeping an apocryphal myth alive as witness the current multi-million dollar business of selling aphrodisiacs based entirely on myth.

Four historians of the sixteenth century are primarily responsible for introducing the fountain of youth myth to the New World and two of them name the search for it as the purpose of Ponce de León's voyage.

The first of these is Peter Martyr, a learned Italian cosmographer and historian at the court of Ferdinand and Isabella, who was a contemporary of both Columbus and Ponce de León. Martyr made it a point to question all the early explorers in order to write his history of the Indies and to develop his map of the New World which we will see in the next chapter. Martyr would certainly have questioned Ponce de León at the time of his return to Spain in 1514 following his discovery voyage.

Figure 6. The European image of the fountain of youth.

Peter Martyr first mentioned the fountain being found in the New World in 1516 in a letter to Pope Leo X. Immediately following the description of the voyage of Juan Diaz de Solis, he stated, "Among the islands north of Española is one called Boyuca (Boiuca), alias Agnaneo, which has a notable fountain, and from drinking of its waters the aged are rejuvenated." Being acutely aware of the listening ears of the Inquisition, Martyr hastily added that he did not believe this story since "only the Lord has the power to restore life." Martyr's letters to prelates and his friends in Italy were published in Martyr's *Decades de Orbe Novo* in 1530.

Martyr's letter, written in Latin and subject to various interpretations, has been seen by some scholars as a report of Ponce de León's voyage to substantiate his search for the fountain of youth, but the facts just don't add up to this conclusion. For one thing, even though the letter was written two years after he interviewed Ponce de León, the report is tied instead to the voyage of Solis. Though Martyr located the fountain in the islands north of Española, through which Ponce de León had explored, he did not associate it with the search for the island of Beniny. Martyr certainly would have known that the King's patent clearly spelled out Beniny (not Boyuca or Agnaneo) as the destination of Ponce de León's voyage three years earlier. In fact, we will find in Chapter 2, that Martyr had identified the island of Beniny and shown its location (which Ponce de León was to use in his quest) as early as 1511 without a mention of the fountain being on it. This clearly shows that Martyr's report of the fountain being on the island of Boyuca or Agnaneo (and not Beniny) came from either Solis or some unknown source and cannot be associated with Beniny or Ponce de León's voyage.

The next historian to mention the fountain was Gonzalo Fernandez de Oviedo y Valdés who published his *Historia General y Natural de las Indias* in 1535. Oviedo primarily covered the four voyages of Columbus and gave many details of natural history and government administration in the Indies. He did mention the fountain in passing and was the first to state that this was the purpose of Ponce de León's voyage. Oviedo obviously had a rather jaundiced opinion of Ponce de León since he spoke of his vanity in seeking the fountain of youth as a cure for "el enflaquecimiento del sexo," or sexual impotence.

And it was this one unfounded and unsubstantiated remark of Oviedo which started the ball rolling, wrongfully injecting this fictional Big Lie so firmly in our history books!

Oviedo, in another unsubstantiated and fictional Big Lie, stated that the Indies were first discovered by a Visigoth navigator from Spain centuries before Columbus. So you can see he re-wrote history the way he thought it ought to be rather than the way it really was. And Oviedo's history was written long after Ponce de León was dead and buried so the conquistador couldn't object or set the record straight. Oviedo's false and degrading remark about Ponce de León's sexual prowess hardly stands up to the history of his active "macho" life as a conquistador and the son of a father who had sired twenty-one illegitimate offspring, so it clearly smacks of being a politically inspired slap at the powerful León family who were rivals of Oviedo for court favors.

However, Oviedo was the official historian appointed by the Crown so his tendentious and error-filled history has been regarded as authentic. Naive historians have faithfully copied and quoted (and even embellished) this falsehood in all subsequent histories down to the present time.

Nearly three decades later came the Spanish historian Lopez de Gómara who wrote his *Historia* about the New World in 1550. Gomara really let his imagination run wild and reported both the European myths of the fountain of youth and Amazon warriors as actually being in existence in the Bahamas. Listen to the fictitious garbage which Gomara put in his *Historia* to please his superstitious Spanish readers, "north of Cuba and Haiti lie the Bahama Islands, known as the Lucayans. The natives, first contacted by Columbus on October 12, 1492, when he landed at Guanahaní, or San Salvador, were whiter and more graceful than the aborigines of either Cuba or Hispaniola. The women were so strikingly beautiful that men came from Florida, Yucatan, and even Tierra Firme to seek their favor and live among them. These foreigners attracted by the island sirens contributed to a great diversity of language and an elevation of manners and culture. It is from there that the report comes of Amazon women and a fountain that restores old men."

Gómara's report is obviously fictitious nonsense and is completely at odds with known historical facts of the Taino Indian people and their culture in the Bahamas. Gómara does not directly link this "fountain" with Ponce de León's voyage but since Ponce de León was seeking his island of Beniny in the northern Lucayans (Bahamas), Gómara's spurious report has been used by later historians to erroneously provide that unfounded link.

Quoting Lopez de Gómara, Garcilaso de la Vega mentions Ponce de León's voyages in the first book of his account, called *The Florida of the Inca,* which deals with the explorations of Hernando de Soto. Garcilaso stated that Ponce de León sought a fountain which rejuvenates the aged. He also said that Ponce de León's second voyage (either in 1515 or 1521, Garcilaso was not sure when) ended tragically as everyone died. Ponce de León's "misfortune was to be a heritage for those who succeeded him" wrote the Inca historian, probably in the 1570's.

Next comes the historian Antonio de Herrera who published his history commencing in 1601 which contained the summary of Ponce de León's log. Herrera, writing eighty years after the event, inserted numerous comments of his own that were not in the original log and this has caused some consternation among scholars in trying to sort out which are Ponce de León's words or which are Herrera's inserted words. All the way through the voyage and in the detailed accounts of the encounters with the Indians in Florida there is no mention of a fountain of youth or miraculous spring.

It is only in the summary at the end of the seven months long voyage that Herrera inserts his comment that Ponce de León did not find the miraculous spring that he was seeking. In this instance Herrera was just repeating the erroneous reports of his predecessors Oviedo and Gómara, augmented by the patently fictitious reports of Hernando de Escalante Fontaneda, because he had no way or inclination to refute them. But in doing so he just added one more report which historians can cite to keep this historical falsehood alive.

I mentioned that Herrera's source for linking the fountain of youth to Ponce de León's voyage came not from his log but from later reports by Oviedo, Gómara, and Fontaneda. I've covered the historians Oviedo and Gómara before, but who is this Fontaneda who has now entered the scene as an authority on Ponce de León's voyage? Herrera quotes him extensively in his history. Is he a valid source for obtaining true information about Ponce de León's voyage? Hardly!

Hernando de Escalante Fontaneda was shipwrecked on the Florida Keys as a youth about 1549. Probably because of his youth (thirteen years old) the Indians didn't murder him as they did most shipwrecked sailors. Fontaneda lived among them for seventeen years until at age thirty he was finally rescued by Menéndez de Aviles in 1566. One sixteenth century document states that Fontaneda was rescued by Jean Ribaut in the Cape Canaveral area, but the rescue by Menéndez appears to be the most authentic. Fontaneda was of noble blood, the son of Garcia Escalante, a conquistador from Cartagena. His noble heritage was to serve him well when at a later date he wrote the memoirs of his life among the Indians which were widely circulated in Spain at the time.

Fontaneda spiced up his memoirs by asserting that it was the Jordan River in southern Florida that Ponce de León was looking for in order to "earn greater fame or become young from bathing in such a stream." "Jordan River" indeed! This is just a clever reference to the river in which John the Baptist gave "re-birth" to the early Christians and would appeal to the religiously fanatic Spaniards of the time. Fontaneda adopted the same derisive tone as Oviedo when he stated, "it is cause for merriment that Juan Ponce de León went to Florida to find the river Jordan." There never was a "Jordan river" in southern Florida and Fontaneda knew it, and Ponce de León was not looking for it!

This shrewd and imaginative writer could not possibly have had first hand knowledge on what Ponce de León was looking for since he was shipwrecked as a youth thirty-six years after Ponce de León's voyage. Yet his ridiculous and spurious testimony was accepted by Herrera as historical fact and has been inanely repeated by historians to this day.

Fontaneda also reported a "migration" of Indians from Cuba to Florida early in the sixteenth century whom he alleged were looking for the "miraculous waters" sought by Ponce de León. "Migration" indeed! This movement of the Indians did in fact occur, but these were Indian slaves who had escaped from the inhumane and harsh treatment of their Spanish overlords in Cuba and were given refuge in south Florida by the Calusa Indians. Earlier Ponce de León encountered one of these Spanish-speaking Indians on the southwest coast of Florida and correctly stated that he must have escaped from Española. While I can understand the reason for the good patriotic Spaniard giving this false reason for the so-called migration, I absolutely cannot understand why so many well educated contemporary historians continue to quote Fontaneda verbatim on the reason for this migration as though it is historical fact. They have thus unwittingly lent more support for this false and spurious report of an Indian fountain of youth.

My argument for refuting Herrera's report that Ponce de León was seeking the fountain of youth on Beniny is based on the postulated fact that it is a later insertion by Herrera and was not in the original log. While Oviedo's spurious remark is easily identified as fiction, it is not that easy in the case of Herrera's summary of the log. At the very end of the account, referring to Ponce de León's last ditch effort to find Beniny by sending Ortubio and Alaminos to search for it, Herrera has this to say: " . . . he (Ponce de León) wished to do it himself, because of the account he had of the wealth of this island, and especially of that particular spring so the Indians said, that restores men from aged men to youths."

That certainly seems to say that Ponce de León was looking for a fountain of youth on Beniny, but are those Ponce de León's words or Herrera's inserted words? Notice that Herrera said, "he (Ponce de León) wished to do it himself." Those are the words of Herrera's predecessor Oviedo (parroted by Fontaneda) who said it was Ponce de León's personal vanity that led him to seek the fountain. Then Herrera in this third person summary at the very end of the voyage (the only place he mentions the fountain) said, "so the Indians said," while he might just as well have said, "so Oviedo said the Indians said," or "so Fontaneda said the Indians said." We will see later that in the long and detailed account of the seven month long voyage in which there was a total of five Indian guides involved, there is not one mention of the Indian guides either reporting or being asked about the rejuvenating fountain!

I am not the first to propose that the Indians did not have a legend of a fountain of youth and that this was not Ponce de León's goal in his voyage. Leonardo Olschki of John Hopkins University wrote a detailed treatise on the subject in 1941. Olschki, a linguist intimately familiar with sixteenth century Spanish documents pertaining to the subject, first showed that an Indian legend of a fountain of youth did not exist. He then found evidence in the interpretation of Herrera's text which throws a shadow on his reporting that the goal of Ponce de León was to find an Indian fountain of youth. Some scholars postulate that the Indians may have invented the fountain story in order to induce the Spaniards to leave in search for it. In commenting on this unlikely story, Olschki has this to say, "sly as these natives may have been, it is inconceivable that a man of the experience and boldness of Ponce de León should have fallen into the trap." I agree.

Not pretending to be a linguist, I base my case on the fact that neither Ponce de León or the five Indian guides are reported as mentioning the fountain during the seven months long voyage. Herrera's inserted remark about it at the very end merely parrots Oviedo's and Fontaneda's spurious remarks nearly word for word.

Fray Bartolomé de Las Casas had written a comprehensive history of the Indies prior to the histories of both Oviedo and Herrera. Las Casas lived with the Indians on Española and Cuba for many years as a missionary and was fluent in their language. His history reported in detail the life style, customs, religion, myths and folklore of the Indians but made no mention of an Indian myth of a fountain of youth. It can be argued that because Las Casas didn't mention an Indian legend of a fountain of youth doesn't mean that they didn't have one. However, here we must realize that Las Casas was a well educated cleric and as such would have been fully acquainted with the Prester John and other European myths of the fountain and, knowing the interest in it by his fellow Spaniards, would certainly have reported it if such an Indian myth existed.

It may have been that the romantic image of Ponce de León owes more than a little to a book originally published in 1831 by Washington Irving, entitled *Voyages and Discoveries of the Companions of Columbus*. Irving was in Spain when he became aware of original source documents such as Herrera's History. Eight chapters in Irving's book deal with Ponce de León. The fountain of youth myth is stressed as the hidden reason for his voyages, and Ponce de León is presented as a romantic who failed in his quest, as unusual among conquistadors as was Irving's own creation, Rip Van Winkle, in the lore of New York State.

There has been a proclivity among historians down through the years to accept previously published historical events without question unless they can produce a valid document which will refute it. How naive can a historian be to believe that a young (thirty-nine years old) healthy conquistador would spend a small fortune buying, provisioning, and paying the crews of three ships, obtain a patent from the King to search for what was said to be a rich island, put his mistress aboard (this will be shown later), and then go off on a seven months long grueling voyage to chase down the rumor of a fountain of youth! Yet we find that almost without exception our leading historians faithfully repeat and embellish this falsehood without examining the source documents with a critical and discerning eye.

An example of this is in Samuel Eliot Morison's discussion of Ponce de León's voyage which I quote in part, " . . . going ashore wherever he saw signs of a native village to inquire about the rejuvenating fountain." *Every case reported in the log* where Ponce de León put men ashore it was to get firewood and water and trade with the Indians, hopefully for gold. *There is not one single mention of inquiry about the rejuvenation fountain,* yet Morison has faithfully put these untrue words in Ponce de León's mouth just as did Oviedo, then Herrera and all historians to follow. In like manner Morison, with his unfounded rationalizing, arbitrarily changed the spelling of Martyr's island of Boyuca to Bimini in a strained effort to misquote and force the words of Martyr to say that the fountain was on Beniny (Bimini).

I have made a strong case for stating that the Indians did not have a fountain of youth legend and yet in the same breath have enumerated the statements of several Spanish explorers where they state the Indians told them of such a fountain or "miraculous waters." There is a valid explanation for this seeming contradiction. The early Spanish explorers made no effort to learn the language of the Indians so the Indians were forced to try to interpret what these Spaniards were asking them. With their limited Spanish vocabulary (which certainly would not contain such esoteric words as "miraculous" or "rejuvenating") it is not surprising that when the Indians were asked the location of a miraculous fountain of water which could rejuvenate old men, they would merely suggest the location of one of the numerous fresh water springs in Florida, or even name an island which had abundant sweet water. From this the gullible Spaniard would think (and report) that the Indian was telling him about a fountain of youth!

It is significant that every Spaniard who related what the Indians told him put the fountain or spring or river in a different location and gave a different name. Just this fact alone should indicate to to the reader that the Indians didn't know what the Spaniards were talking about, so their answers were meaningless.

I said that the early explorers did not attempt to learn the language of the Indians and that is true of the explorers but not of the clerics who followed them. As I indicated in discussing the *Historia* of Fray Bartolomé de Las Casas earlier, many of these dedicated missionaries became fluent in the Indian languages, yet there is not one single instance of these learned clerics telling of an Indian legend of a fountain of youth. Doesn't that tell us something? So there we have it. The fountain of youth was not an Indian myth, but an Old World myth transplanted to the New World, and Ponce de León was certainly not looking for it when he discovered Florida.

If Ponce de León was not looking for the fountain of youth, just what was he looking for? Read on and you will find the answer.

2

The Search for the Island of Beniny

After Columbus landed on the island of Guanahaní (the present island of San Salvador) in the Lucayans (Bahamas) in 1492, he immediately turned south. His subsequent explorations in all four voyages were well south of that point. In like manner, the official recorded explorations of the Spanish explorers who followed Columbus up to Ponce de León's time, had been well south of Guanahaní. How was it then that Ponce de León, in preparing for his voyage in 1512, said that he had "news that they had discovered lands to the north"?

A number of historians have speculated that Ponce de León was at that time referring to John Cabot's discovery of Newfoundland in 1497, but I doubt it. That certainly qualifies as "lands to the north" but it's just too far north. Ponce de León must have heard about something closer to home but still north of Guanahaní which was the most northerly known island in the Spanish discovery area.

Although there were no officially recorded Spanish explorations north of Guanahaní, there was one highly publicized unofficial Spanish exploration voyage said to have taken place in 1497. This fits the bill perfectly for furnishing Ponce de León his "news" of the reported but unexplored "lands to the north."

Enter that charming faker Amerigo Vespucci. Vespucci was a Florentine aristocrat who resided in Seville and was in the merchant banking and ship chandlery business during the Spanish exploration period. He furnished supplies to many of the early explorers including Columbus on his third voyage. Amerigo was a colorful and fluent writer and it was this skill, together with his unmitigated egotism and shameless disregard for the truth, that was to propel him into an unearned and undeserved role as the discoverer of new "lands to the north."

Vespucci first went to sea with Alonso de Ojeda in 1499 as a gentleman volunteer (another way of saying a paid passenger). He wrote an inspired and vivid account of this voyage to the Indies and return, in which he never mentions Ojeda and pictures himself as both the captain and the navigator, performing these duties with exceptional skill and courage. With the recent advent of the printing press, accounts such as this by a popular and well-bred aristocrat received wide distribution and thus assured Amerigo instant fame as an accomplished (alleged) sea captain and navigator.

With that false fame and reputation tucked firmly under his belt, Vespucci had no problem signing on two Portuguese voyages in 1501 and 1503 to explore the newly discovered shores of Brazil. These voyages were captained by the veteran and able Portuguese seaman Gonçalo Coelho. Amerigo is rather contemptuous of Coelho on these voyages, never mentioning him by name, but claiming that his own superior knowledge was the only thing that saved the fleet. Listen to what he has to say on the subject, "though a man without practical experience, yet through the study of the marine chart for navigation, I was more skilled than all the ship masters of the whole world." What an overblown ego! The amazing part of this whole charade is that the king and most of the court believed him.

The accounts of these three voyages are interesting enough, but it was the account of a fictitious voyage which he says he took in 1497 that literally put Amerigo's name on the map. This voyage which never took place is also the basis for Ponce de León having "news that they have found lands to the north."

In this alleged voyage of 1497, Amerigo claims to have been the first to discover the mainland of the New World by landing on the north shore of Brazil (conveniently one year before Columbus landed in 1498). His account of this voyage so impressed Martin Waldseemüller, a young college professor and cartographer in Lorraine, that he placed Amerigo's portrait and his newly discovered (alleged) coastline of the mainland as an insert on Waldseemüller's now famous map of 1507.

On this map Waldseemüller also placed the name "America" on the mainland (derived from Amerigo to make it sound more like a continent) and since cartographers had been searching for a name for this new continent, it quickly spread throughout Europe. When it was later discovered that our genial fraud Amerigo had been active in his ship chandlery business in Seville during the entire year of 1497, the name America had become set in concrete so we are stuck with it instead of Columbia which it rightfully should be.

But we are concerned with the "lands to the north" which interested Ponce de León and these are clearly shown in Figure 7 which is a scaled copy of the insert on Waldseemüller's 1507 world map.

Notice how the shores of the mainland north of Hispaniola and Cuba look surprisingly like the Yucatan peninsula, the Gulf of Mexico, Florida and the east coast of the United States, even though our history books tell us these were to be discovered and explored at a much later date. This fact has led Amerigo's faithful advocates and champions to insist that he really made that fantasized voyage. Like some other charismatic charlatans, he still has some devoted followers despite his obvious chicanery.

There is an explanation for the seemingly accurate shoreline depicted by Amerigo. It could have come from one or several illegal and unpublicized exploration voyages which he could have exploited because of his position as Piloto

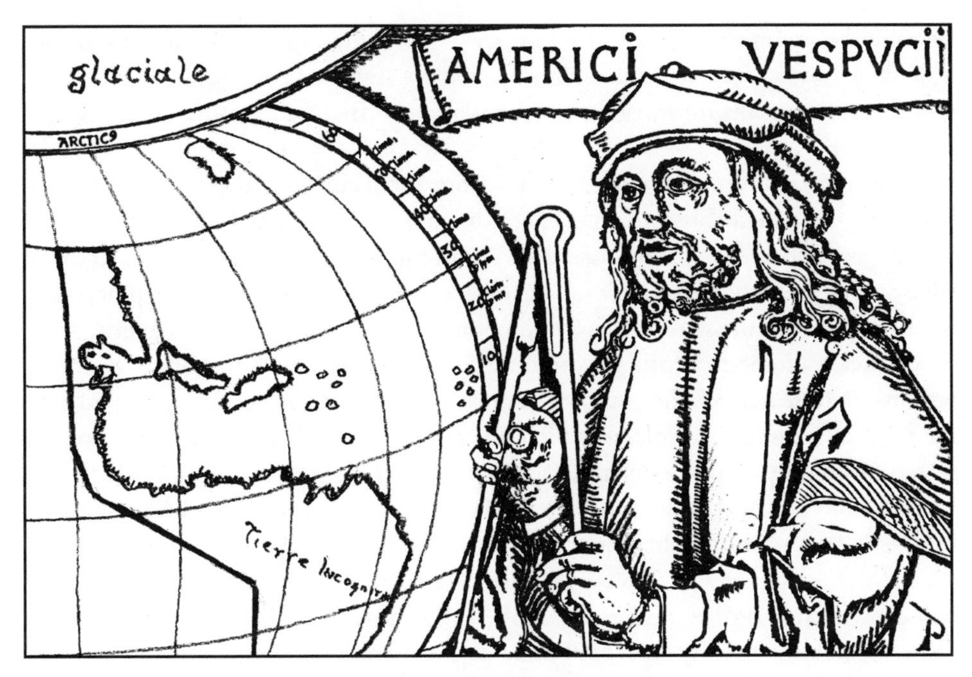

Figure 7. A scaled copy of an insert from Martin Waldseemüller's world map of 1507.

Mayor. Amerigo was appointed as Spain's Piloto Mayor in 1508 because of his then apparent (but false) reputation as a world experienced navigator. The Piloto Mayor was responsible for the licensing of all blue water pilots or navigators and for maintaining the official "padrón real" or official world map for the archives of Spain. In this capacity, Amerigo would have had access to informal and secret information from pilots of both Spain and Portugal (through spies) who had made unofficial and unrecorded slaving or exploratory voyages to the unexplored shores of the New World.

Amerigo could then take this privileged information and appropriate (steal would be a better word) it for his own use in charting the shoreline of his fake 1497 voyage. But for our purposes it really isn't necessary to determine the exact source or validity of these published shorelines. It has been suggested that they came from Amerigo's vivid imagination and just by coincidence conformed to the actual shoreline. I find this hard to believe and prefer my explanation, but the important point is those "lands to the north," whether valid or not, would have been known to a considerable number of people in the early sixteenth century from Amerigo's published account of his alleged voyage and from Waldseemüller's 1507 world map.

It is doubtful if Ponce de León would have had a copy of either Amerigo's published account of his voyage or Waldseemüller's map, but the "news" of these discovered lands would have been brought from Spain by the captains and the pilots of the supply ships constantly arriving in the Indies and Ponce de León would certainly be among the first to eagerly seek this "news" from the homeland. So now we know where Ponce de León obtained his "news of lands to the north," but where did he get his information on the island of "Beniny" that he named as his goal?

Ponce de León had apparently heard from the Taino Indians that the lands to the north contained this immensely wealthy and more civilized island of Beniny. This report about the wealthy island of Beniny must have been common knowledge among the other Spaniards in Española as well, so there was a certain urgency in moving fast on this voyage before someone else beat him to the discovery.

In fact, Columbus' brother Bartolomé had also approached the King requesting permission to search for the island of Beniny. In a letter dated 23 February, 1512 to the royal officials in Española, in which he granted permission to Ponce de León to search for Beniny, King Ferdinand had this to say, "I think that he (Ponce de León) has reason to be content, because the Adelantado don Bartolomé Columbus talked to me here that he wished to discover this island (of Beniny). I believe he (Bartolomé) might have discovered it with better advantage to our treasury than we will do with Juan Ponce de León." This clearly shows that there was competition for the search for Beniny and that Ponce de León was given preferential treatment over any of the Columbus family.

In the patent granted by the King, Ponce de León had three years to accomplish the task, dating from the time he signed the contract. The expenses of the expedition were Ponce de León's, as were the costs of constructing any houses or estates in the colony-to-be. Building and administration of forts was reserved to the King. Ponce de León was given the title of Adelantado of Beniny which was extended to any other nearby lands he might discover for twelve years. Ponce de León would receive the conquistador's tenth of all revenues and profits from the new colony, a perquisite which would have expired before 1530. Ponce de León was forbidden to include any foreigners in his expedition. The Crown would distribute Indians already resident in Beniny to the colonizers with preference given to Spaniards who made the trip with Ponce de León.

We will find later that Ponce de León was convinced that the wealthy island of Beniny which he was seeking was somewhere in the northern Lucayans (Bahamas) northwest of Guanahaní. The Indians would certainly not have pictured Beniny in the northern Bahamas because they knew that the land there was no different from their own and peopled by Indians just like themselves. Then where did Ponce de León get his information about the location of Beniny?

Here we return to Peter Martyr, the court historian who was the first to report the fountain of youth myth in the New World, but did not connect it to Ponce de León's voyage. Peter Martyr published his *Legatio Babylonica, Occeanea Decas, Poemata, Epigrammata*, in Seville in 1511. This document was a description of the New World and contained a rather crude and somewhat distorted map of the New World and its relation to the western shores of Europe. It is this map that we are

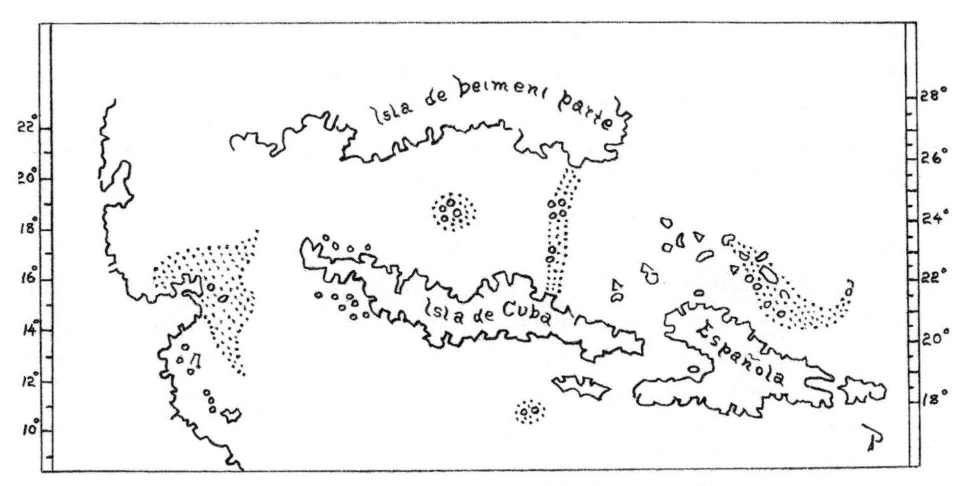

Figure 8. A portion of Peter Martyr's 1511 map of the New World.

now interested in because it contains the European source for Ponce de León's "Island of Beniny" and shows its location in relation to Puerto Rico and the Lucayans (Bahamas) through which he was to sail.

An accurately scaled reproduction of the northeast portion of Peter Martyr's map is shown in Figure 8. The projected latitudes not present on the original map have been added and are based upon extrapolation from known landmarks. While most of Martyr's map is grossly distorted, this northeast portion shown is fairly accurately portrayed since this was the area of most intensive occupation, exploration and charting at the time.

The "Isla de Beimeni Parte" shown in the upper or north part of the map is the "Island of Beniny" named by Ponce de León as his goal in the official patent from the Crown and sought by him in his exploration voyage. In other charts and documents of the time, this elusive island is spelled variously as Beniny, Beimeni, Bimenei, and finally the modern Bimini. Variation in spelling of place names is common in this early exploration period, but all refer to the same island. This map not only indicates the island of Beniny but shows Ponce de León how to get there.

Again referring to the map, you will find Puerto Rico (Ponce de León's departure point) in the lower right hand corner, east of Española and between 18 and 19 degrees latitude. Then north and west of Puerto Rico are the Bahamas and the Turks and Caicos islands, known then as the Lucayans. The island at the extreme northwest end of the island chain at 24 degrees latitude is Guanahaní, Columbus' landfall and at which point he turned south for his further exploration. Much of this map would have been made from Columbus' charts which would have been available to Martyr and thus these charts would have shown Guanahaní as the northernmost island of the Lucayans charted by Columbus.

I said that the map shows Ponce de León how to get to his island of Beniny and indeed it does. You can follow his route easily. From Puerto Rico (the unmarked island on the map east of Española) he must sail in a northwesterly direction, through the shallow banks in the southern Lucayans (shown with the dotted area). Then staying in the open water just east of the Lucayans, but keeping them in sight, he would arrive at the northernmost island of Guanahaní. Guanahaní then becomes his jumping off place for the open water hop in a northwesterly direction to Beniny (Beimeni on the map). And that's exactly what he did as will be shown in the reconstruction of his sailed track.

It is doubtful if Ponce de León had a copy of this map, but he wouldn't need it as long as he had a general idea of what was on it. And since this map represents the latest knowledge available at the time of his planned voyage, it becomes a graphic picture of the "news" of which he spoke. It clearly shows Beniny (Beimeni) located in a northwest direction from Guanahaní. Ponce de León was an aristocratic conquistador and not a seaman or navigator so, from this knowledge of where he wanted to go, he would turn over the mechanics of getting there to professional seamen and pilots (navigators) whom he could well afford to hire for the job.

Ponce de León's patent required him to undertake this voyage at his own expense so he set about outfitting and provisioning three ships, and hiring his crew in the early months of 1513. He provisioned for a long voyage so no doubt carried livestock to be slaughtered along the way for fresh meat. He must have done a lot of cooking aboard as at every opportunity he would send men ashore to gather firewood. A Spanish conquistador would be lost without his horse for either battle or parade so he took his mare along although there is no indication she was ever ridden. In addition to the officers, the crew in each ship would have consisted of able bodied seamen, ship's boys (apprentice seamen), soldiers, and to keep the vessel seaworthy and afloat, ship's carpenters, riggers and caulkers.

His fleet consisted of two caravels, the "Santiago" and the "Santa Maria de la Consolación," and a bergantina, the "San Cristóbal." We have no record of the size of these vessels, but judging by the size of the crew and the amount of provisions that would be necessary, I would place the caravels at between seventy-five to eighty feet in length and the smaller bergantina between fifty to sixty feet in length. Figures 9 and 16 will give you an idea of what these vessels looked like.

The two caravels would have been square rigged forward with a lateen sail aft. The bergantina was probably rigged with two lateen sails with provisions for converting the forward mast to a square rig as conditions might dictate. Many of the shallow draft bergantinas were equipped with long sweeps or oars to facilitate movement in shallow rivers and bays so the "San Cristóbal" would have been an ideal addition to this exploration fleet.

Ponce de León's flagship was the caravel "Santiago." Diego Bermúdez (his brother Juan discovered Bermuda) was master, and Antón de Alaminos served as chief pilot. Alaminos came over with Columbus on probably his second voyage (there is conflicting evidence as to which one) and stayed in the Indies to become one of the most experienced and sought after pilots in the islands.

Figure 9. The 1513 vessels of Ponce de León.

Alaminos had with him two Taino Indian guides familiar with the islands which was common practice with the early Spanish explorers beginning with Columbus. As I have indicated earlier, the Taino Indians were a seafaring and trading culture who ranged far and wide in their large trading canoes so these Indian guides knew the islands well. But as we will see later there was a problem in conveying this knowledge to the Spaniards due to the language barrier.

The flagship "Santiago" also had aboard some very interesting passengers. These were Francisco de Ortega, a "gentleman of the land," his wife Beatriz Jiménez, and Juana Jiménez, probably Beatriz's sister or cousin. The report of these passengers on the voyage is contained in letters and documents uncovered by Morison in his extensive research into the Spanish archives. Some scholars might question whether they were really aboard since they are not listed on the extant ship's manifest. This only indicates a misunderstanding of the pure accountability purpose of an official sixteenth century ship's manifest which listed only those people who were either directly the responsibility of or were accountable to the crown. Ortega and his family fall into the same category as did the 200 aristocrats (including Ponce de León) reported by Oviedo to have been with Columbus on his second voyage who likewise are not listed on any of the seventeen ships' manifests.

This is the first reported instance of females of noble blood being aboard a Spanish explorer's ship so Ponce de León is breaking a precedent. Ortega, his wife Beatriz, and the maiden Juana are reported as being aboard at the start but that is the last we hear of them for the entire voyage. With a long and arduous exploration voyage ahead of him, why would Ponce de León burden himself with an unproductive landsman passenger accompanied by two equally unproductive females?

This question has been glossed over or ignored by all previous historians, but I refuse to push it aside because the answer to the question has a significant impact on the controversial purpose of the voyage. I don't have to be clairvoyant to answer this question! The rational, logical and overwhelmingly obvious answer is simply this: *Juana Jiménez was Juan Ponce de León's mistress!*

This was Ponce de León's voyage. He paid for everything, and with an official patent from the king, had complete control over who could or who should be aboard the "Santiago." So why wouldn't he take his mistress along? Herein lies a problem because strictly enforced Spanish custom of the times would not permit the unmarried gentle maiden Juana Jiménez to go unless she was properly chaperoned by one of her own family. This then is the reason for having the landsman Ortega and his wife Beatriz Jiménez aboard as passengers. Ponce de León no doubt told Ortega and the women that they would enjoy the voyage (I doubt that they did) so why not come along for the ride?

Before I undertook my research voyage to reconstruct Ponce de León's 1513 exploration voyage, I studied all previous historical writing that I could find on the subject. There have been a number of shallow tourist-oriented books or pamphlets written on Ponce de León, but I found that the number of significant works by valid historians is very limited. However, there has been a limited effort by some recent historians to document and report Ponce de León's voyage in a historically factual manner. I found with dismay that these recent accepted historical publications were filled with errors. The foremost of these is the monograph, "History of Juan Ponce de León's Voyage to Florida," by T. Frederick Davis, published by the Florida Historical Society in 1935. This is a complete, well documented study and analysis of the voyage which contains charts of his postulated route. The only problem is that Davis' charts and findings are completely wrong as will be shown later in this text.

An oft quoted document is a pamphlet by Edward W. Lawson and Walter B. Fraser, *The First Landing Place of Juan Ponce de León on the North American Continent,* privately published in 1956. This deals only with Ponce de León's initial landing site in Florida. As a historical document it is tainted by being an unabashed public relations piece promoting the fountain of youth tourist attraction in St. Augustine.

The next entry into the field is the chapter on Ponce de León's voyage in Samuel Eliot Morison's *The European Discovery of America: The Southern Voyages,* published in 1974. Morison's treatment of the subject is filled with conjecture and fiction which makes for interesting reading but not true factual history. A postulated (and inaccurate) chart of the route is included, also based entirely on conjecture rather than hard navigational data.

The Spanish historian Eufemio Lorenzo Sanz has a chapter on Ponce de León in his history of the Spanish conquistadores which covers a projected landfall on the Florida coast. Unfortunately this work has never been translated into English so is unavailable to the lay public.

The most recent report is the chapter on Ponce de León in Robert S. Weddle's book, *Spanish Sea,* published in 1985. This primarily consists of comments on previous historical writings including those above. He spends an inordinate amount of time dwelling on strained and irrelevant documentation of the fountain of youth myth and accepts Morison's flawed track of the voyage.

My findings on the historical facts of Ponce de León's voyage differ markedly from those gentlemen referenced above. In following and analyzing Ponce de León's navigation log to determine where he touched land, the problem is primarily one of navigation and marine geography. These are two specialized fields of endeavor in which most academic historians are sadly lacking in experience. However, in those subjects I can point to my fifty years experience as a professional navigator of aircraft and ocean sailing vessels together with my intimate geographical knowledge of the route of Ponce de León's voyage, as I have sailed extensively in the islands and Florida waters for nearly thirty years.

So now I will take you along on my research voyage. By precisely following Ponce de León's log I was able to duplicate his voyage and touch land in the same places where he made his several significant discoveries. But first bear with me while I explain the methodology I used to be sure that my voyage would exactly duplicate the track of Ponce de León's vessels through the islands and to the several landfalls on the coast of Florida and Cuba.

Most historians arrived at Ponce de León's landfalls by pure conjecture based upon a cursory examination of the compass headings given in the log. The few who have plotted his course on a chart have done so without taking into consideration the effect of the strong currents encountered or the effect of early sixteenth century magnetic variation on the actual compass heading that was sailed. My scientific and empirical method of arriving at the true track, by using a sailing vessel to retrace the voyage, takes these factors into consideration and is thus superior to the plotted tracks of theoretical navigators.

At first glance it might appear that a sailing vessel to duplicate the voyage of Ponce de León should be a square-rigged wooden vessel about the same size and shape as his vessels, but such is not the case. The basic requirement is for a submerged sailboat hull that will move through the same waters at the same speed and thus be acted upon by the currents to the same degree. What the topsides (the hull above the waterline) and the sail plan look like is completely irrelevant. In like manner the hull should have enough depth and wetted surface (drag) to react to the currents in a similar manner and these factors cannot be judged by size and configuration alone.

The vessel used as a test vehicle in this research voyage was a Southern Cross, a heavy displacement, full keel, double ended cutter from the board of Thomas Gilmer, a naval architect noted for his designs of traditional seaworthy vessels. This traditional hull form of a deep draft, full keel vessel with an outboard rudder dates back to the English Channel cutters of the 1800's which in turn were developed

Figure 10. The sailing yacht "Gooney Bird."

over the years from the English cog, a vessel contemporary with the caravels of Ponce de León. While topsides, sail plans, and construction methods have changed drastically over the years, the underwater hull form of a traditional heavy displacement sailing vessel has changed very little since the fifteenth and sixteenth century. Thus my Southern Cross cutter named "Gooney Bird" (after the Air Force C-47 airplane with that nickname) would react to the ocean currents to the same degree that Ponce de León's caravels did and made a perfect research vessel to re-sail and duplicate Ponce de León's voyage.

"Gooney Bird" has other attributes that makes it a superb research vessel. It has all the latest state of the art navigation equipment allowing me to plot an accurate course as sailed. I have one primary and four backup electronic autopilots that can steer a given course better than I can. I have customized it for long ocean passages so it carries more than normal fuel, water and stores, allowing me to stay at sea for the long periods necessary in my research duplicating the long voyages of Columbus and Ponce de León.

I have said that I customized "Gooney Bird" in order to "duplicate" the long voyages of Columbus and Ponce de León. But believe me, I'm duplicating only the navigation track or path that they sailed and not trying to duplicate the rather Spartan life the Spaniards lived aboard their vessels. I have a four burner propane stove with an oven and broiler instead of cooking in an iron pot over a wood fire burning in a sand box on deck. My meat products are from cans rather than slaughtering livestock as I go. Most of my fish also comes from cans (I'm big on sardines), but I do occasionally put a fishing line over the side which I'm sure Ponce de León's crew did constantly. My one concession to more closely duplicate their life style is that I don't have refrigeration or ice aboard so I have to drink my rum "neat" as the English sailors would say.

One of my biggest problems in loading provisions and stores aboard is to provide ample stores of cat litter and cat food for the official ship's cat, a female tabby named "Hooker," the only other crew member aboard. Hooker eats primarily the dried cat food that comes in bags with an occasional treat of canned fish cat food. She supplements this diet with flying fish that she gathers up off the deck as they come aboard at night.

To duplicate Ponce de León's track in "Gooney Bird" I must sail the compass headings from the log at the same speed as Ponce de León's vessels did to be sure that the currents will influence the track to the same degree. I also sailed the voyage in the summer (1990) to ensure that I was sailing in similar wind and current conditions. This speed was easily computed from the time he took to cover a known distance, but the compass headings given in the log must be corrected for magnetic variation conditions then prevailing before they can be used to sail or plot the course today. I realize some of this detailed technical discussion can become tedious, but it is necessary to assure an accurate re-sailing and reconstruction of Ponce de León's voyage.

To make these necessary corrections to the compass headings, I drew upon the data furnished me by James E. Kelley Jr., a respected historian of early seafaring and navigation and a colleague of mine in the international Society for the History of Discoveries. Kelley developed the early sixteenth century magnetic variation for the area from a brilliant computer analysis of early charts, maps, rutters, and other documents.

Another factor requiring compass correction is the fact that compasses of the time were made in various European cities and it was common practice for the compass to be set to true north when manufactured. This built into the compass the magnetic variation correction for that city. Kelley has also deduced from a study of early maritime navigation that the Spanish explorers of the period were using a compass made in Seville with a 1/2 point (5.63 degrees) easterly correction built in. This correction (I should say error) built in by the manufacturer had the effect of having the north arrow on the card point to the left, or counterclockwise, 5.6 degrees from magnetic north.

So then on a voyage when *magnetic north* is moved further to the left or counterclockwise as in a westerly variation zone, the north arrow on the card will also be rotated to the left or counterclockwise from *true north* to the degree of the westerly variation. Accordingly I have applied this 5.6 degree correction of the Seville compass to my navigational computations. This adjustment of the sixteenth century compass produced a condition which is no longer a problem since modern charts show the difference between true north and magnetic north.

With the means for correcting the log's compass headings at hand, and knowing the speed at which the vessels were sailed, I was then ready to take "Gooney Bird" and, following the log, re-sail Ponce de León's voyage of discovery.

My first task was to get "Gooney Bird" from my home port in Bradenton, Florida, to Ponce de León's starting point in Añasco Bay on the western end of Puerto Rico. This proved to be the hardest part of the entire voyage as I had to beat into the southeast trade-winds and the strong Antilles current for well over 1000 miles. I passed through the Keys at Channel Five near Key Largo (which Ponce de León named "Pola") then getting on the Great Bahama Bank west of Andros Island (discovered by Alaminos in 1513), I sailed south and anchored in the lee of the Ragged Islands to await more favorable winds.

My anchorage was on the "Columbus Bank," so named because Columbus passed the Ragged Islands (he named them "Sand Islands") on his way to Cuba in 1492. Sailing through this area so steeped in early history, I had the almost eerie feeling that I had been transported back into the sixteenth century and every sailboat I saw on the distant horizon seemed to be a lateen-rigged Spanish caravel. After five days the wind veered more easterly allowing me to sail on through the Turks and Caicos Islands and reach Añasco Bay in Puerto Rico in early May 1990 about a month after Ponce de León started his voyage on 3 March, 1513. Ponce de León had earlier departed Santo Domingo on Española (Dominican Republic), but had anchored in Añasco Bay to provision his ships from his extensive nearby plantations. So it is from that point that he began his navigation log which I was to follow in "Gooney Bird."

Ponce de León departed from Añasco Bay on the western shore of Puerto Rico in the afternoon of 3 March, 1513 in his search for the wealthy island of Beniny. Passing Point Aguada (now called Point Borinquen) he took his departure for navigational purposes sometime during the night of 4 March or early morning hours of 5 March. And remember that it is his pilot Antón de Alaminos who is navigating so this is the point at which he would start his dead reckoning (compass course and distance) plot on his portolan chart.

The portolan chart was a large bleached sheepskin upon which the fifteenth and sixteenth century pilot plotted his dead reckoning course. Entries were made with ink but the sheepskin could be scraped clean and used over and over again. And in some ways for a sailing vessel it was superior to our modern paper charts which disintegrate when wet. Knowing that he was going into unexplored territory to the north, Alaminos' chart would be largely blank with probably only the north shores of Puerto Rico, Española and the known Lucayan islands indicated on the lower edge. The remaining blank space was to be filled in from his dead reckoning navigation as they sailed into these unknown waters.

Alaminos would then plot his track from his compass course and distance to fix his position in relation to his starting point at Point Aguada. And it would be from this dead reckoning chart that Alaminos would estimate his latitudes (the number

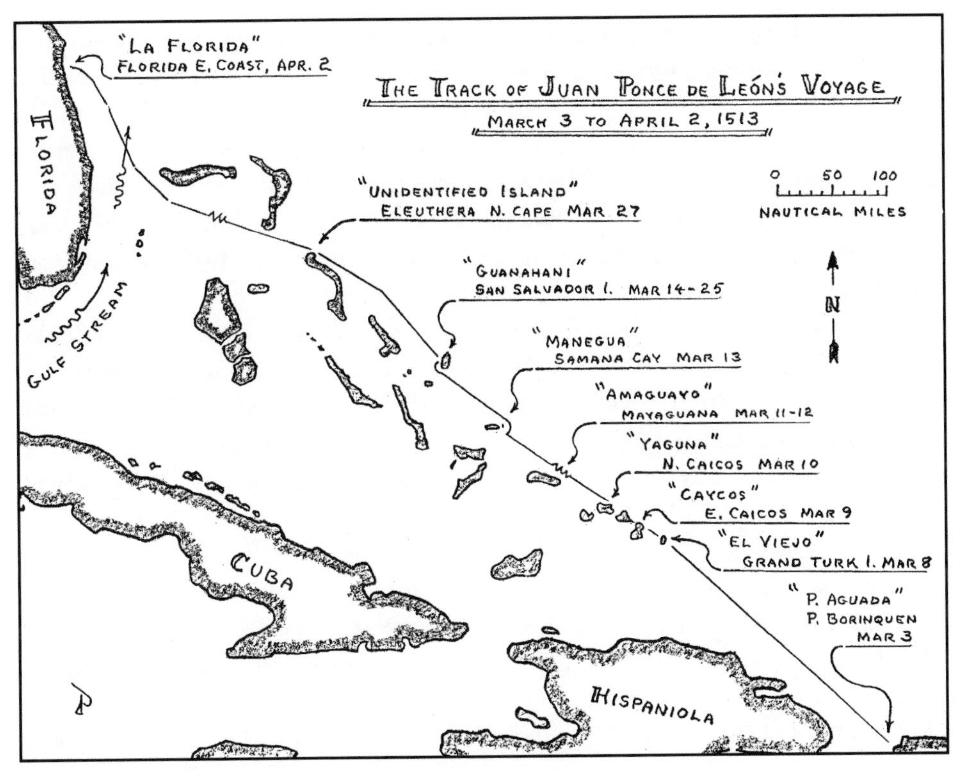

Figure 11. Ponce de León's track through the Bahamas.

of degrees north of the equator) for the islands and Florida landfalls. Remember this point about how the latitudes were determined for it is crucial to the controversy over where Ponce de León landed on the shores of Florida. His resultant plotted track would look much like my plotted sailed track in Figures 11 and 12.

From Point Aguada, Ponce de León set a course of northwest a quarter by north and sailed for 3½ or 4 days (the log is not clear on the exact hours sailed) over open water until: " . . . they came to anchor at the banks of the Babueca, at an island that they call El Viejo, which is in twenty-two and one half degrees (latitude)." Correcting the course given in the log for both the magnetic variation that prevailed, and for the built-in Seville compass variation correction, I duplicated that leg of the voyage by sailing on a heading of 316 degrees at a speed of 2.6 knots. This may seem like a rather slow speed, but it is entirely reasonable for these clumsy heavy laden vessels. My sailed track shown in Figure 11 was bent considerably to the west of the 316 degree heading by the branch of the strong Antilles current which flows westerly past Hispaniola and Cuba. After sailing a little less than four days I made landfall on Grand Turk Island located at the north end of the Turks Island Bank.

Ponce de León said he anchored on the "Banks of the Babueca" and indeed the wide shallow Turks bank stretches almost 20 miles in a southwesterly direction from Grand Turk. Grand Turk is one of several smaller islands in this general area which is located on a large bank (Babueca). Since it is the largest it would be the one where Ponce de León would anchor to obtain provisions. Grand Turk is thus identified as "El Viejo" from a geographical standpoint as well as through my navigation of the log. Babueca, which has an Indian name, would certainly have been known to the Indian guides and was probably on Alaminos' chart as well. And, referring back to Peter Martyr's map we see the bank pictured (the dotted area) with Grand Turk (El Viejo) shown correctly at the northeast end.

Both the "Banks of the Babueca" and the island of "El Viejo" were no doubt on Alaminos' chart as there is strong evidence that Martín Alonzo Pinzón in the "Pinta" discovered them in 1492. This discovery by Pinzón was made during that period in late November 1492 when he broke away from Columbus to go looking for gold on his own. Las Casas, in his *Historia de las Indias,* reports that Pinzón sailed along a bank which the Indians called Babueca and gave one of the islands on the bank (probably the largest, Grand Turk) the Spanish name of "El Viejo." Columbus would have put this information on his charts and this in turn would be made known to Alaminos and other Spanish pilots of the period.

The log gives the latitude of "El Viejo" as 22 degrees, 30 minutes, while the actual latitude of Grand Turk is 21 degrees, 25 minutes (from the anchorage on the bank south). This placement of the latitude a little over one degree too far north will be reflected to some different degree in all later latitude reports in the log. The reason for this is quite obvious as Alaminos started his dead reckoning from Point Aguada with a northerly error on his chart. This is quite understandable since all early sixteenth century charts and rutters (navigator's guide) consistently showed known landmarks in the New World as several degrees too far north.

You recall that I said Martyr's map showed Ponce de León how to sail along the east edge of the Lucayans (Bahamas) to Guanahaní the northernmost island, before hopping off over open water to Beniny (Beimeni on the map). That is exactly what he did then and I am going to follow him now. So for the next six days until he reached Guanahaní Ponce de León was island hopping along the eastern edge of the Lucayans. He would barely leave one island astern when he would pick up the next island on the horizon. He anchored at night when he could find an anchorage. And I was able to do the same in "Gooney Bird." This does not require the precise navigation which is necessary on the long passages out of sight of land. The next several islands are identified primarily by being either a day or overnight sail from the last island as indicated in the log. This island hopping track is shown in the chart in Figure 11.

After leaving the anchorage at El Viejo, the log reads, "the next day they anchored in an islet of the Lucayans called Caycos." From the chart it is clear that this is East Caicos, an easy day's sail of about twenty-five miles. This is one of the few islands to have retained the Indian name to this day.

This was the really pleasant and enjoyable part of the voyage in "Gooney Bird." The long overwater legs of the voyage require me to constantly monitor my compass heading and speed. At frequent intervals I record my over the bottom track so I can accurately plot Ponce de León's track on the chart at a later date. That's just plain hard work. After a few days those waves all begin to look alike and I found myself scanning the horizon for a sail or palm tree or anything to break the monotony. Not so while I'm just island hopping among these semi-tropical islands where I can relax and enjoy the view like any tourist on a cruise ship. At the end of a short pleasant day of sailing through these crystal clear waters anchoring in a secluded cove opposite a white sand beach provides the perfect setting for my happy hour. I trust Ponce de León enjoyed this part of the voyage, too, because there would be harder times coming.

At this point the log reads, "soon they anchored at another called Yaguna in 24 degrees." This can easily be identified as North Caicos, again an easy day's sail of about 35 miles as indicated by the expression "soon they anchored." The north shore of North Caicos is at latitude 21 degrees, 58 minutes north, indicating that Alaminos is carrying forward the northerly error from his departure point with the error gradually increasing. This increase in error can be explained in part by the fact that Alaminos was unaware of the increasing westerly variation bending his compass heading to the south and so he would have thought he was traveling on a more northerly course.

Ponce de León then continues on his way to Guanahaní and " . . . at the 11th of the same (month) they came to another island called Amaguayo, and there they stayed 'al reparo.'" As the chart shows, sailing in a northwesterly direction for about 48 nautical miles, an easy overnight sail at 2.6 knots, brings them to Mayaguana. Most scholars in previous works have said that they anchored here for "repairs," but that is completely wrong. In his translation Kelley has correctly shown that "al reparo" means hove-to or, as in Columbus' log, "jogging on and off." I hove-to in "Gooney Bird" in the same manner that Ponce de León would have done in his caravels. This requires reducing sails to the minimum and strapping them in tight, then lashing the tiller so the boat quarters into the wind and the waves, barely maintaining steerage at about one knot or less.

From Mayaguana they sailed to an island called "Manegua" which they apparently passed by without stopping and reported that it lies at 24 degrees, 30 minutes latitude. As the chart shows, this is clearly Samana Cay whose latitude is 23 degrees, 03 minutes, once again showing that Alaminos by his dead reckoning is retaining his original northerly error.

This is the small, barren, and uninhabited cay which the National Geographic Society has named as "Guanahaní" the landfall island of Columbus, but Ponce de León does not arrive at Guanahaní until the next day and about 65 miles further along the northwesterly course. Who is correct here? Ponce de León says Samana Cay is "Manegua" (and early sixteenth century cartography agrees) but the

National Geographic Society says it's "Guanahaní." I'll opt for Ponce de León since he had two Indian guides with him who certainly could correctly identify both "Manegua" and "Guanahaní." The National Geographic Society, without benefit of Indian guides, was forced to come up with a tortured and contrived reconstruction of a portion of Columbus' navigational log to justify naming Samana Cay as Guanahaní.

Ponce de León passed by Samana Cay without anchoring, and I know why. A suitable and safe anchorage just doesn't exist on Samana Cay for vessels the size and draft of Ponce de León's caravels. In 1987 when I made an analytical study of Columbus' 1492 discovery voyage (including a re-sailing of his route from his log), I approached Samana Cay from the east in "Gooney Bird" to see if it would conform to Columbus' geographical description of his landfall island. It not only didn't conform to Columbus' geographical description, but I could not find Columbus' anchorage or the "great harbor" he found on the north end, and the reason is they simply do not exist on Samana Cay.

I made one more attempt to find an anchorage site during this voyage in 1990, watching my depthometer and poking into shore within a few hundred feet of the reefs that surround the cay and again could not find a shelf suitable or safe for either Columbus or Ponce de León to anchor their caravels. Yet the theoretical navigators of the National Geographical Society have shown on their chart of Samana Cay an anchorage where an anchorage does not exist!

So now we will leave the National Geographic Society on Samana Cay desperately defending their flawed and discredited theory that it is Guanahaní, and rejoin Ponce de León sailing northwesterly from Manegua (Samana Cay) seeking Guanahaní, where he will hop off in the search for his island of Beniny. The log at this point reads, "at the 14th they came to Guanahaní, which lies in 25 degrees, 40 minutes (latitude), where they trimmed up one ship in order to cross the windward sea of those islands of the Lucayans." He then identified the island as the one that "Christoval Colón" (Columbus) discovered.

Alaminos reports the latitude of Guanahaní as 25 degrees, 40 minutes when it is actually 24 degrees zero minutes, once more showing that Alaminos was determining his latitudes from his dead reckoning chart and thus carrying his original northerly error through the entire voyage. It is interesting to note that later in the voyage Alaminos reports that Key West and the adjacent keys lie at 26 degrees, 15 minutes, while the Keys actually lie at 24 degrees, 35 minutes, so his northerly error at that known point was one degree, 40 minutes, about the midpoint or average of his northerly errors. Then if we take that one degree, 40 minute average northerly error and subtract it from his report of Guanahaní lying at 25 degrees, 40 minutes, the result would be a latitude of 24 degrees, right through the middle of San Salvador!

In both my 1987 and my 1991 re-sailing and reconstruction of Columbus' discovery voyage, I ended up at San Salvador to pinpoint it as Guanahaní, the island of

Columbus' landfall. Now with the identification of San Salvador as Guanahaní from both Ponce de León's and Columbus' logs, we have what in navigation parlance is referred to as a positive fix (when two tracks from independent sources cross each other). So Ponce de León has made his first significant discovery in this voyage by naming the Bahamas island of San Salvador as Columbus' landfall in the New World.

You recall I pointed out that the Peter Martyr map (Figure 8) shows Guanahaní as the last or most northern island in the Lucayans from which to hop off across the open sea in a northwesterly direction to Ponce de León's island of Beniny (Beimeni on the map). And Ponce de León clearly infers that is just what he is doing by staying there nine or ten days and making the boats ready to cross the "windward sea."

Guanahaní at this time was apparently uninhabited, the entire Taino Indian population having been wiped out by the rapacious slave raiders within two decades from the time Columbus first set foot on the island. What a sad commentary on the start of European occupation of the New World, that the first gentle people who welcomed us were the first to be destroyed.

Ponce de León is the last recorded visitor to Guanahaní for some hundred years and in Bahamas history, this time is referred to as "the silent period," when the islands lay largely if not totally uninhabited. The next inhabitant of Guanahaní was the English pirate John Watling who made the island his base of operation in the early seventeenth century. The ruins of his plantation-type buildings, known as Watling's Castle, still stand on the southwest corner of the island. Guanahaní became known as Watling's Island at that time and the name lasted until 1926 when the Bahamas government officially gave it back the name of San Salvador, as it had been named by Columbus in 1492.

"Gooney Bird" is a familiar sight in the anchorage at San Salvador, as I visited there on numerous occasions during my Columbus voyage research. By far the most memorable occasion was on Columbus Day, 12 October, 1992 (the Quincentennial or 500th anniversary of Columbus' landing and discovery of the New World). I had just completed a re-sailing of Columbus' voyage from Palos, Spain (his departure port) via the Canaries, to San Salvador to celebrate this historic event.

On this voyage I departed Palos on 3 August (exactly 500 years after Columbus), then departed Gomera in the Canaries on 6 September (exactly 500 years after Columbus) and with good winds I arrived at San Salvador five days before Columbus and so was there on Columbus Day, 12 October, 1992 for this historic Quincentennial Celebration. "Gooney Bird" was the only vessel which re-sailed Columbus' voyage from Spain on the exact 500th anniversary. You may hear of others who will make this claim, but they left from different ports at later times so theirs were not true re-sailings of the voyage as was mine.

Now back to Ponce de León in his search for his fabulous island of Beniny. Having readied his ships for crossing the open sea to Beniny, Ponce de León set sail from Guanahaní on a northwest course probably sometime during the day of 25 March. On 27 March, after sailing two days, they sighted an island which they could not identify and they did not stop to examine it so continued on their way. They no doubt could not identify it because it wasn't on their chart which probably ended at Guanahaní. And the fact that Ponce de León did not stop to explore this island means that it did not resemble what he had heard about the island of Beniny, so he must have considered it just another poor and uninteresting island of the Lucayans (which it was indeed).

Ponce de León's northwest heading of 315 degrees when corrected for the Seville compass factor and for the magnetic variation in the area becomes 300 degrees so that is the true heading I sailed in "Gooney Bird," at a speed of 2.6 knots to duplicate his track. My track was pushed north by the strong Antilles current in this area and ran about 15 nautical miles east of Cat Island, then ran into the northwest trending coast of Eleuthera. This track (see Figure 11) shows that Eleuthera was the island "they could not identify" and they would have followed the coast and rounded it to the north at Bridge Point and resumed their northwest heading. I did the same in "Gooney Bird" and this put me in a position which surprised me somewhat.

The postulated tracks of nearly all previous research in this field show Ponce de León rounding Great Abaco as the island they saw but could not identify. This track is a natural conclusion because the long chain of Bahama islands lies in a generally northwesterly direction, and this is the last island before an open space across to the shore of Florida. Up to this point I had assumed my track would do the same so when my sailed track ran into Eleuthera far south of Great Abaco, I thought my whole project was in trouble because of bad course correction factors.

But these factors had worked well for over 700 miles and in pinpointing six of the islands scattered through the Bahamas, so why would they fail now? Also the log clearly states that Ponce de León sailed on a northwest heading when leaving Guanahaní and there is no way you can bend that northwest heading around to reach Great Abaco. That is when I realized that Great Abaco was not the turning point toward Florida. It had to be Bridge Point on Eleuthera.

On Monday, 28 March, Ponce de León had left Bridge Point on Eleuthera astern and resumed his northwest course toward Beniny. At this time Ponce de León would have thought he was in the open sea and indeed he sailed out of sight of land for the next six days until making landfall on the shore of Florida. It is the precise duplication of this six day sail that is crucial to determine just exactly where Ponce de León landed on the shores of Florida. And it is on these long overwater legs through strong currents affecting the track that my use of a sailing vessel to duplicate the track is far superior to the work of the theoretical navigator using non-empirical and suspect data to arrive at his track.

The log entry at this point reads, "they ran 15 leagues by the same course, and Wednesday they proceeded in the same way." This means that for two twenty-four hour sailing days they ran northwest 15 leagues (about 45 miles) each day. The speed computes out to less than two knots (1.87). I believe this reduced speed is deliberate. Alaminos and Ponce de León are now sailing into unknown, uncharted waters. They had already been surprised to see an unknown and uncharted island. This was not the time to rush headlong forward and perhaps end up on a reef, so I believe they intentionally slowed their progress, constantly sounding with the lead, and possibly they hove-to at night or in times of restricted visibility, especially since they were sailing into a period of dark nights with a waning moon.

To maintain this reduced speed I sailed "Gooney Bird" with drastically reduced sails. Sailing the corrected heading of 297 degrees, I found that the strong Antilles current carried me right through the wide New Providence channel about 10 miles south of the southern cape of Abaco. Since they had seen Eleuthera in daylight, they would have passed the cape of Abaco after dark, but they could not have seen this low island 10 miles away even in daylight. The track from Eleuthera to the coast of Florida is shown in Figure 12.

My sailed and reconstructed track passed within the mathematical sighting range of both Cat Island and Great Abaco, but I did not see either island, and neither did Ponce de León. Yet I find that theoretical navigators constantly use this purely mathematical theoretical sighting range to determine or prove at what distance a sailor is able to see an island at sea.

The theoretical sighting range is based upon a mathematical projection of a viewer's line of sight passing just inches over the curvature of the earth's horizon and picking up the top few inches of the highest elevation on an island in unlimited visibility. Far more than the top few inches of an island must be above the horizon for the naked eye to see it, and unlimited visibility never exists in the Bahamas, especially during the summer months when a heavy sea haze is present. For this reason, the theoretical sighting range is completely irrelevant here so even though my chart appears to show Ponce de León sailing through a maze of several islands, he was unable to see them and thought he was in the open sea headed for Beniny.

Herrera condensed his summary of the log entries from 29 March to 2 April into one short sentence following the two day, 90 mile, run from Eleuthera. During this period, Ponce de León ran into a storm and was forced to change his desired northwest heading to west-northwest. At this point (29 March) the log reads, "and afterwards, with bad weather, up to 2 April, running west-northwest, the water (depth) decreased to 9 brazas (approximately eight fathoms), at one league from shore."

A careful reading of the log at this point indicates that on 29 March they ran into a cold front passage with the accompanying storms and a wind shift to the northerly quadrant forcing them to change course to west-northwest. During the initial passage of the front when the wind would have come out strong from the

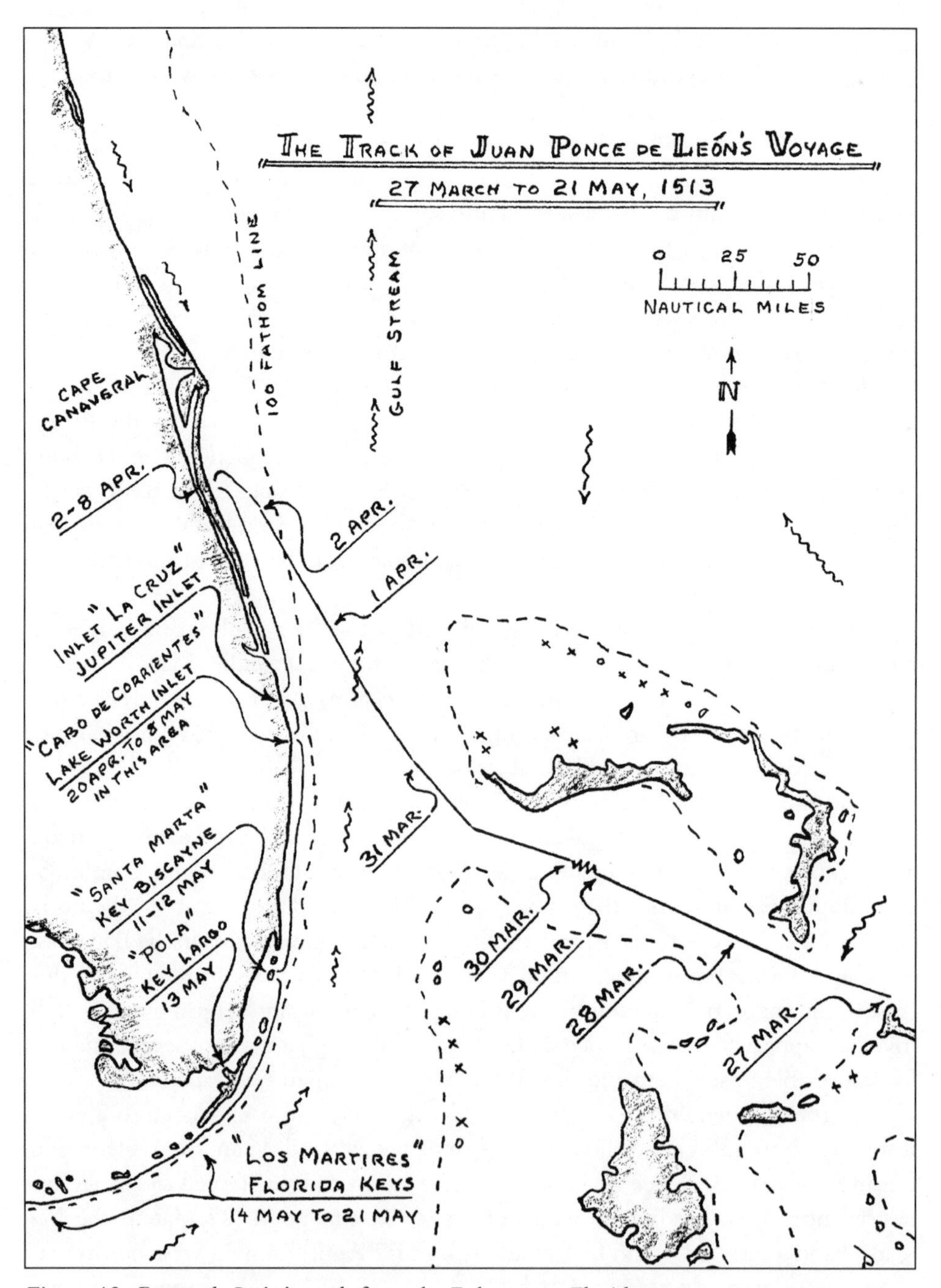

Figure 12. Ponce de León's track from the Bahamas to Florida.

northwest and north during the storms, they would do what any prudent sailor would do so they hove-to or jogged along barely moving under reduced sail. Only after about twenty-four hours when the winds would have shifted to the northeast and the storms abated would they be able to pick up that west-northwest heading and resume their voyage. Lacking a convenient frontal passage and storm, I simulated this action in "Gooney Bird" and this is reflected in the track shown in Figure 12.

With this new heading of west-northwest, they would be hard on the wind rather than running with the wind as before. Since a square-rigged vessel of that era simply does not like windward work, their forward progress would be reduced to a crawl. This, combined with their cautious jogging at night would reduce their forward progress to about thirty miles a day or less. Accordingly, I reduced the speed of "Gooney Bird" to the same degree to exactly duplicate the track of Ponce de León's vessels over the bottom.

The Spanish vessels would be crossing the Gulf Stream at its strongest point where it is squeezed between the lower eastern bulge of Florida and the protruding Great Bahama Bank. In this venturi it can and does pick up speeds of well over 3 knots. With the slow progress of the vessels through the water at this point, they would be swept north faster than their progress west during this twenty-four hour plus period and this is reflected in the track. These strong currents gradually built up at an ever changing rate until they peaked at 3.8 knots in midstream, then gradually lessened as "Gooney Bird" (and the Spanish vessels) neared the Florida coast. This produced the curved "S" shaped true track over the bottom shown in Figure 12.

Anyone with even a rudimentary knowledge of navigation should realize that this scenario of constantly changing (and unknown) currents would be virtually impossible to program into a computer or plot manually with any reasonable degree of accuracy. This fundamental fact proves that my sailed empirical reconstruction of the track is far superior to any artificially plotted track by a theoretical navigator using suspect estimated data.

Early on 2 April as they reached the 100 fathom line and moved out of the strongest current, the track began to veer more westerly and they would have reached their landfall and subsequent anchorage later that day. After landfall Ponce de León ran along the coast looking for an inlet or harbor, and not finding one he anchored offshore in eight "brazas" (about forty-four feet) of water. The log is ambiguous as to whether he ran along the coast in a northerly or southerly direction, but the question is moot since he could not have gone far before nightfall forced him to anchor. At my projected site, based on the log, the description of the coastline fits, and the depth of water for the anchorage is within a few feet of that reported.

From my sailed and reconstructed track I found that Ponce de León's anchorage (and subsequent landing) was at 28 degrees N. latitude and 80 degrees 29 minutes W. longitude, which is below Cape Canaveral and a short distance south of Melbourne Beach. I am not so naive as to say this is the exact spot, but I would place the accuracy within five to eight nautical miles on either side of this navigational fix.

Ponce de León went ashore the next day to take possession of his newly discovered land and the log carries this notation, "and believing that this land was an island, they named it La Florida, because it was very pretty to behold with many and refreshing trees, and it was flat, and unvarying: and because moreover, they discovered it in the time of the Feast of Flowers (Pascua Florida)."

Many accounts of Ponce de León's landing say that it occurred on Easter Sunday which is responsible for the name, but that is wrong. Easter Sunday in 1513 was on 27 March, the day they had sighted the unidentified island. The Spaniards tended to stretch out their religious holidays into longer periods or "seasons" so Ponce de León's landing on 3 April was well within the Easter season known as Pascua Florida.

Ponce de León tried later to obtain the Indian name for this new land with confusing and almost ludicrous results. His Taino Indian guides thought he was asking about the local Indian population so they gave him the Indian term "cautio" which Ponce de León reported was the Indian name of this new land. But at a later date and with later knowledge, Herrera was to report that "the Indians said that it (Florida) was called Cautio, the name that the Lucayan Indians gave to that land, because its people have their secret parts covered with palm leaves woven as a plait."

We can be thankful that Ponce de León named this new land La Florida before he learned the Indian name for it and called it Cautio. How would the beautiful state of Florida ever live down the ignominious reputation of being named after an Indian jock strap?

In describing this new land Ponce de León said "it was very pretty to behold with many woodlands and was level and uniform." The woodlands have fallen to the axes of the first settlers, but the description of level and uniform land geographically fits my landing site perfectly. He reported no Indians or Indian villages and no inlet or harbor. That also fits the site since it is located on a long low spit of land only a mile or so wide and separated from the mainland by a wide lagoon. A nice place for beach condominiums but hardly a place for an Indian village.

I stayed at anchor here for two days to get a bit of rest and catch up with my paper work in accurately logging and recording Ponce de León's exact track across the Gulf Stream to his landing on the coast of Florida. The previous 72 hours had been hectic and tiring because of the steady flow of freighters and cruise ships in the area. This compelled me to stay on deck and keep a watch whenever any vessel was in sight and on a possible collision course. I was only able to sleep in 20 to 30 minute catnaps when no boats were in sight. I perhaps shouldn't use the expression "catnap" because Hooker slept soundly through the whole episode.

Now let's return to Ponce de León and the goal of this voyage, namely his search for the island of Beniny. Here we have an enigma. I have shown from Peter Martyr's map how the island of Beniny (Isla de Beimeni) can be reached by sailing northwest across the open sea from Guanahaní. And we have seen that Ponce de

León prepared his ships on Guanahaní for that overwater passage and then set forth on a heading of northwest. Then, after sailing nine days towards Beniny, he lands on what he believes to be an island that is in exactly the place Beniny should be. Now what?

Does Ponce de León at this time declare with some exuberance, "I have found the grand and wealthy island of Beniny!" Of course not! This low monotonous coastline with not a soul in sight just does not fit his mental picture of what Beniny should look like, so he gives it a pretty name and continues on in the search for his elusive island of Beniny.

Now just what was his mental picture of Beniny? Here we find that Beniny, Beimeni, or Bimini, is an Indian name, and so the description of the grandeur and wealth of the island (or land) would have come from the Indians. And where was this wealthy and exotic land that the Indians were referring to? Certainly not in the northern Lucayans or Florida. The Indians would know full well that this area contained no gold and was inhabited by simple people like themselves. Where then would it be? The answer to this is so obvious it literally slaps you in the face!

This wealthy and exotic land that the Indians were describing was the realm of the Indian civilizations on the mainland, accessed by the Yucatan peninsula! Here the Indians would describe high mountains filled with gold, large cities with houses made of stone, magnificent temples roofed with gold that seem to reach to the sky, and grand princes who ruled over exotic people who wore clothes and were advanced in the arts and sciences. This is the land the Indians described to Ponce de León. This was the image Ponce de León had in his mind of his elusive island of Beniny. Small wonder then that he dismissed the shores of Florida as just a low and uninteresting island and continued on his search.

You recall I said the Taino Indians were a seafaring and trading culture who traveled throughout their islands and the mainland as well. Recent archaeological digs in Taino Indian village sites have revealed artifacts from both Mexico and Central America. So the Taino Indians would be familiar with the grandeur and wealth of the various civilizations on the Yucatan and elsewhere on the mainland. Yet, with their simple and limited vocabulary, the problem was getting all this across to these obstinate Spaniards who could think of nothing but gold and islands. We have seen earlier how this same communication problem between the Spaniards and the Indians produced the false notion that the Indians knew about a fountain of youth and were telling the Spaniards about it.

Columbus had the same communication problem nearly two decades earlier in his first voyage when he asked the Indians of Española about the source of their gold. In Columbus' log of 11 December 1492, the Indians were clearly telling him about Mexico and the Yucatan, but Columbus wrongly assumed it was just another nearby island. Look at what the Indians were saying about this land, and I quote the Indians in part directly from Columbus' log. " . . . (v)ery great with very large mountains, rivers, and valleys," " . . . larger than Cuba," " . . . not surrounded with

Figure 13. A Mixtec chief in his palace.

water," " . . . behind this Española and of infinite extent," and " . . . harassed by an intelligent race." And later the Indians said that, in this land, the people were clothed and it was a ten day canoe trip away.

The Indians were clearly not telling Columbus about just another one of their islands "surrounded by water," but were describing the Maya on the Yucatan and the mainland of eastern Mexico, harassed by the intelligent race of Aztecs. The Indians must have told Ponce de León something similar but he, like Columbus before him, assumed the Indians were talking about another one of their islands and so wasted his time looking for the wrong thing in the wrong place. We will see later in the voyage that the Indians once again tried to tell Ponce de León about the Yucatan, but it simply didn't register.

Now let's get back to Ponce de León standing on the beach after his landing on the coast of Florida and see if we have put him in the right place. I have shown that Ponce de León made landfall and subsequently anchored and went ashore at about 28 degrees latitude in the vicinity of Melbourne Beach, Florida. This does not agree with the writings of earlier historians who have placed his landing elsewhere. Let's examine these previous proposed landing sites and test their validity against historical, navigational, and geographical facts.

The foremost historian to make a detailed study of Ponce de León's voyage, including an analysis naming his landing site, was T. Frederick Davis in his monograph published by the Florida Historical Society in 1935. This scholarly paper places the landing site a short distance north of St. Augustine inlet at about 30 degrees, 08 minutes, latitude. Davis supports this site with a chart showing the track from Great Abaco to the landing, and also with a discussion on how Alaminos arrived at his reported 30 degrees, 08 minutes, latitude.

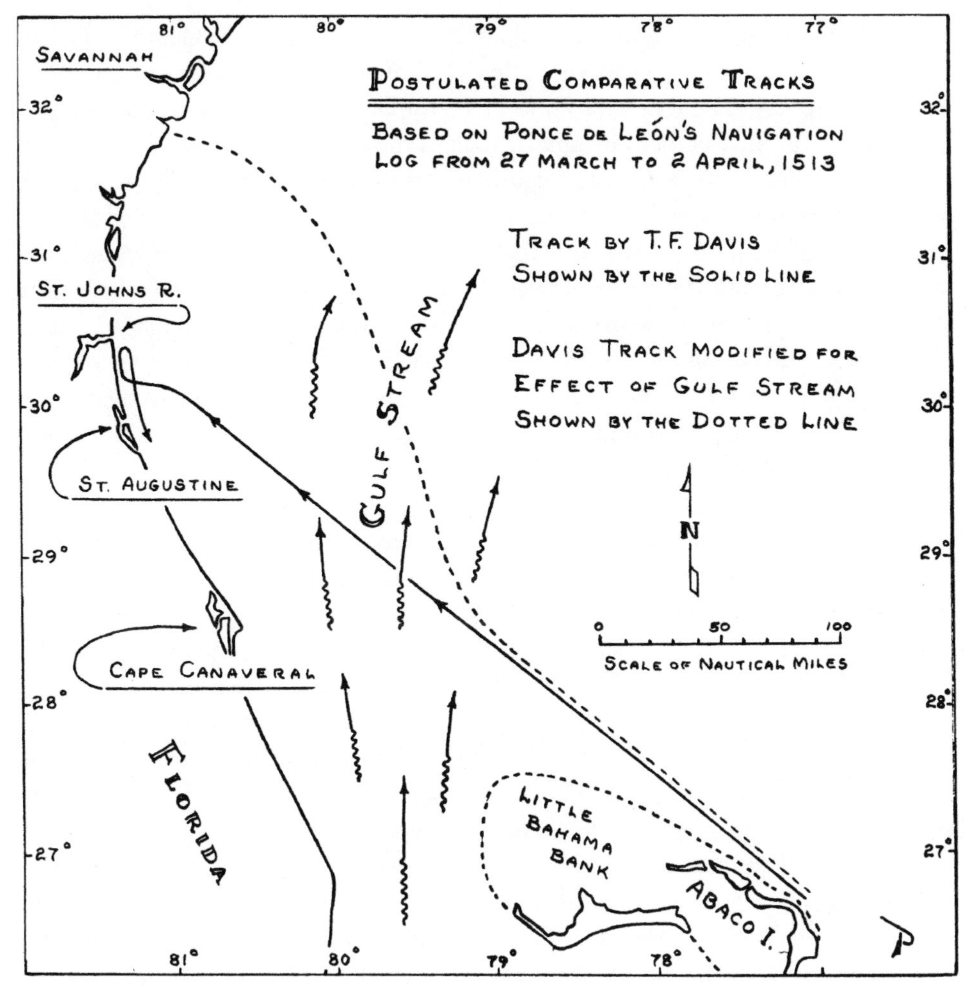

Figure 14. The corrected T. Frederick Davis track.

First let's examine Davis' chart and see if it depicts Ponce de León's track from Great Abaco in an accurate and factual manner. A careful scrutiny of Davis' track reveals that it cannot possibly be an accurate and true depiction of Ponce de León's track because it is a straight line drawn on the chart in a northwest direction without regard to the effect of the strong Gulf Stream current. You recall how the Gulf Stream bent my sailed track drastically to the north from the sailed northwesterly heading, and certainly the same thing should have occurred to Davis' postulated and plotted track from Great Abaco.

Accordingly I have computed the effect of the Gulf Stream current on Davis' track and have shown this on the chart in Figure 14. On this chart Davis' track (scaled from the chart in his paper) is shown as a solid line. My recomputation of his track, taking into account the Gulf Stream current, is shown as a dotted line. You will note that the dotted line, which is the actual track that Ponce de León's vessels would have followed, puts the landfall a little south of Savannah, Georgia. This is well over 100 nautical miles north of Davis' landfall from his unrealistic and inaccurate theoretical straight line track. So much for Davis' theoretical navigation plot, but what about his argument for the latitude of the site?

Davis seems to have a strong argument for his landfall site in that it is at 30 degrees, 08 minutes, which is the exact latitude reported by Alaminos. But to support that argument he must show that of the ten latitudes given by Alaminos, which Davis readily admits are between one and two degrees too far north, this one, and only this one, was an accurate noon meridian celestial navigation sight. He supports this incongruous theory with what at first glance appears to be a learned though convoluted explanation of sixteenth century celestial navigation as practiced by Alaminos. But under close scrutiny we find that his explanation is neither learned or true.

To begin with, he lists all ten of Alaminos' latitudes and then without any substantiation, boldly announces that "only one, the 30 degree, 08 minute, landfall of Ponce de León on the Florida coast (at St. Augustine), has the 'earmarks' of a carefully obtained instrumental reading." What are these "earmarks"? He doesn't say. And then he has Alaminos obtain that one alleged "carefully obtained instrumental reading" by use of a cross staff to sight the noon meridian of the sun.

The cross staff or balestila was adapted to marine navigation and first put into use by Dutch navigators around 1529. It was slow to be adopted by the rest of Europe and even Verrazzano and Cartier, decades after Alaminos, didn't have one. Yet Davis puts one in the hands of Alaminos in 1513 and then asks us to believe that Alaminos had the knowledge and expertise to use it.

For Alaminos to find latitude from the sun meridian would have required use of the sun declination tables in a then current *Regiomontanus Kalendarius*. These documents, written in Latin, were intended for and used by learned astronomers, mathematicians, and cosmologers who could compute latitude from the sun's height by using the data from the tables of declination in a spherical geometric equation. To suggest that a simple, unlettered, up from the ranks, Spanish pilot like Alaminos could do this (even if he had a cross staff) is being naive in the extreme.

Look at what Samuel Eliot Morison, a renowned and respected historian of sixteenth century navigators and navigation has to say on the subject, "celestial navigation formed no part of the professional pilot's or master's training in Columbus' day or for long after his death. It was practiced only by men of learning such as mathematicians, astrologers, physicians, or by gentlemen of education." Alaminos was certainly none of these so we can be certain he used only dead reckoning to determine his azimuth position and latitude. Alaminos' use of dead reckoning to determine his latitudes also explains why they all have a northerly error differing only in degree, which in turn is accounted for by the inexact means he had of determining speed and distance over the bottom in the unknown currents through which he sailed.

We can't rule out the fact that Alaminos was probably familiar with and may have tried to use an early form of celestial navigation. The simple mariner's quadrant had recently come into use by pilots of this era, but with less than satisfactory results. Columbus mentions trying to use one in his 1492 voyage but gave up on it and went back to his dead reckoning. Alaminos may very well have had one aboard, but there is no mention or indication of it being used during the voyage.

In 1987 I made a replica of a fifteenth century quadrant and I tried to use this instrument to determine the latitude on both my Columbus voyages and the Ponce de León voyage. The quadrant (i.e., one quarter of a circle) is a crude forerunner of the more sophisticated sextant used by modern navigators. The quadrant determines latitude by measuring the angular height of Polaris (the North Star) above the horizon by use of a plumb bob or weighted string against the 90 degree index. I tried using the quadrant under ideal conditions both at sea and at anchor. At sea I was generally off my known latitude by as much as ninety miles or more. At anchor I did a little better, but my average error was still about sixty miles. So what's my point? Just this. I have said that there is no indication that Alaminos used a quadrant. However, even if he used one, I have shown that the chances are he wouldn't have come up with latitudes any better than those he determined from his dead reckoning. Figure 15 gives a graphic picture of this quadrant and how it is used.

Davis' landfall site doesn't look very good from a navigation standpoint, so now let's look at it from the standpoint of geography. After leaving his landing site, Ponce de León then sailed slowly south along the coast for twelve days. He reports no inlets, no capes, no Indian villages, until he comes to a cape which he names "Cabo de los Corrientes," and which both Davis and I identify as the cape just north of Lake Worth Inlet. This is consistent with the smooth and relatively barren coast south of my landfall at 28 degrees latitude.

But here Davis is in trouble because the geography south of his landing site does not fit this description in the log at all. Within a few miles of turning south along the coast, Ponce de León would have seen the large inlet and harbor at St. Augustine and also the large Indian village that Menéndez de Aviles later found at that site. Davis peremptorily dismisses this troublesome spot, and with a conviction born of necessity, simply states that Ponce de León was too far offshore to see it. Really now? Ponce de León at this time was looking for inlets and Indians so why would he sail so far offshore that he couldn't see them? And particularly when deep water runs to within a few hundred yards of shore? Then a little later Davis argues that Ponce de León must round the prominent Cape Canaveral without seeing it or entering it in the log, a completely unrealistic (and unbelievable) scenario.

Clearly Davis' landing site north of St. Augustine has failed both the navigation and geography test and so can be eliminated as the true landing site of Ponce de León on the coast of Florida.

I have spent a good bit of time in refuting Davis' landfall and landing site because he is a well known and respected historian of Florida history and his well

Figure 15. The author, using a mariner's quadrant based upon a fifteenth century design.

written and scholarly thesis on the Ponce de León voyage has been largely accepted by the academic community as an accurate portrayal of this historic event. The landing sites proposed by the three remaining historians are of lesser importance and acceptance so will now be discussed only briefly.

Edward W. Lawson, who had previously published a credible biography of Ponce de León, in a later pamphlet produced with Walter B. Fraser placed the landing site inside St. Augustine harbor immediately adjacent to the "Fountain of Youth" tourist attraction. This is not consistent with the log which clearly shows that Ponce de León looked for but did not find an inlet or harbor. Lawson, with the assistance of his navigation advisor Captain William J. Peters, moved Alaminos' reported latitude south to the St. Augustine Inlet by finding an error in the very copy of the sun declination tables that he says Alaminos was using. Lawson and Fraser go to great pains with many footnoted testimonials to show that a large Indian village existed on the site (apparently not realizing that this is an argument against the site) and that the site had an abundant spring of sweet water which from earliest times had been known as the "fountain of youth." Then to cap it off, a buried stone cross allegedly dating to the time of Ponce de León was found on the site. This pamphlet is a commercial promotional publication masquerading as a historical document.

Samuel Eliot Morison follows the track suggested by Aurelio Tío in his article on the Ponce de León voyage and places the landfall site at Ponce de León Inlet north of Cape Canaveral and south of St. Augustine. Morison does not back this up with any navigational data which makes sense and in this I am extremely disappointed since he has done such an excellent job of analyzing the voyages of Columbus, Magellan, Cabot, Verrazzano and others. He has Ponce de León land at an inlet when no inlet was mentioned in the log. Then he contradicts himself, saying he can find no evidence in the log that Ponce de León tried to sail north from his Florida landfall, and in the next paragraph (five lines later) says that after landfall the fleet "sailed the same way, i.e., north." But as I pointed out earlier, Morison's biggest error was in introducing the fiction of Ponce de León inquiring about the fountain of youth each time he went ashore.

The Spanish historian Eufemio Lorenzo Sanz, in his comprehensive history of the Spanish conquistadors, has a chapter on Ponce de León. This chapter primarily concerns Puerto Rico but, in the abbreviated section on the discovery of Florida, he includes a chart showing the track of Ponce de León's 1513 voyage. This track shows the east coast landfall at St. Augustine and the west coast landfall at Tampa Bay. No definitive navigational data is included to substantiate this track.

The most recent historian to pinpoint Ponce de León's landing site is Robert S. Weddle in his book *Spanish Sea*. Weddle follows Morison's lead in placing the landing at Ponce de León Inlet. Weddle falls into the same trap as the others in believing that Alaminos' latitudes came from celestial navigation. He also accepts Great Abaco as the jumping off point for crossing the Gulf Stream without realizing it would be quite impossible to reach Ponce de León Inlet from that point on a northwesterly heading (see Figure 14). However, while we can discredit Weddle's landing site, I would hasten to say the chapter on Ponce de León in his book comprises only a very small part of his excellent and comprehensive history of early Spanish exploration of the entire Gulf of Mexico area.

There you have all the pros and cons of the different proposed landing sites. Now let's return to Ponce de León and follow him as he explores his new found island of "La Florida."

3

La Florida: Fighting and Failure

The historic moment when Ponce de León formally took possession of La Florida for Spain has been romantically embellished by history writers and artists far beyond reality. He is frequently pictured or described as standing in a sea of gaily colored wild flowers, surrounded by well dressed conquistadors and pious looking priests, with a few interested Indians looking on from the sidelines. But it just didn't happen that way! Ponce de León was the only conquistador, the other soldiers were hired mercenaries and probably rather motley looking. There were no priests aboard the vessels, no Indians made an appearance, and alas, there were no wild flowers as they do not thrive in the salt laden air of the eastern shore.

The scene would have been more as the log describes it: a low and level seashore with a view of the native pine and cedar trees, and the ubiquitous cabbage palms in the background. And Ponce de León, disgusted with not finding his fabulous island of Beniny where it was supposed to be, probably hurried the whole affair in order to be on his way in the search for his elusive grand island. It is significant that Ponce de León did not bother to leave one of his inscribed stone crosses at the first landing. It was only at a much later time when he realized the size and extent of his island that he put one on shore. Ponce de León was obviously determined to continue his search for Beniny, but first he decided to explore the shores of this uninteresting island to see if by some chance it contained something of value.

Ponce de León left the anchorage at the landing site on 8 April, and sailed south to start his exploration of La Florida. He sailed slowly south along the shore, no doubt anchoring at night. For twelve days he reports no inlets, no capes, and no Indian villages. As pointed out previously, this scenario is consistent with the smooth and relatively barren coast south of my landing site at 28 degrees latitude, but does not fit the coastline at all for the proposed landing sites north of Cape Canaveral. Sailing "Gooney Bird" about 500 yards offshore in about fifty to sixty feet of water I found an average northerly current of about one knot, which together with the light winds for this time of the year account for Ponce de León's slow progress south.

Then on 21 April Ponce de León made his next significant discovery of this voyage. He discovered the Gulf Stream. And he did it in a rather abrupt and dramatic fashion. As he rounded a cape which he later named "Cabo de los Corrientes" (Cape of the Currents), he ran into a current so strong that it was pushing the boats backwards faster than they were sailing forward even though he said they had good winds at the time. It should be noted that my references to the current off the east coast of Florida as the "Gulf Stream" use the popular term. The correct technical oceanographic term for the current at this early southern point is the "Florida Current." Ponce de León in the "Santiago" and the other caravel were able to anchor just offshore, but the bergantina was caught a little farther out in deep water. Being unable to anchor it was carried back north and out of sight before the end of the day. This action could only have taken place at the bulge (or cape) of the coast just north of Lake Worth Inlet. I experienced a 2.3 knot current when sailing past this point and it could be more if influenced by tidal flow from Lake Worth Inlet.

At this point the 20 fathom line (too deep for anchoring) comes within about one mile of shore and the shallow shelf for anchoring falls off rapidly here, rather than gradually as it does farther north. Under these conditions the third ship could have been within a few hundred feet of the two which were anchored yet it would be unable to anchor and so would be carried north by the current.

This scenario cannot be repeated north of Cape Canaveral as there the bottom very gradually gets deeper, providing ample anchoring depths as much as twenty miles offshore. This is one more factor that completely rules out a landfall above that point since Ponce de León, in following the coast south, would stay in sight of land. The first cape he would come to would be Cape Canaveral where these conditions do not exist.

I said that Ponce de León discovered the Gulf Stream and so he had, but he didn't realize it at the time any more than he realized he had discovered the mainland. No doubt to him it was just that current that kept him from going where he wanted to go and caused him to lose sight of one of his ships. But his pilot Alaminos had noted the current that carried the bergantina out of sight north and was later to use this knowledge to establish the route of the Spanish galleons on their return voyages back to Spain.

In July 1519 when Cortés was in a hurry to get his first shipment of gold from Mexico back to Spain to curry favor with the King, he sent his flagship "Santa Maria" with Alaminos to pilot the ship on the fastest route. Alaminos took the then unused and untried route north along the Florida coast to take advantage of the strong current he had experienced earlier on his voyage with Ponce de León. He then discovered that this current was not confined to Florida but continued for thousands of miles bending eastward and carried him in record time three quarters of the way across the sea to Spain. Thus the Gulf Stream route across the Atlantic was set to be used not only by the gold laden Spanish galleons but by all eastbound shipping to this day. And it all started with Ponce de León's first encounter with the then unnamed Gulf Stream at "Cabo de los Corrientes."

Now let's return to Ponce de León anchored near shore where he has encountered the Florida Indians for the first time. While anchored near "Cabo de los Corrientes," Ponce de León noticed some Indians on the beach beckoning him to come ashore. Thinking this was a friendly gesture and a good opportunity to learn something about the island, he took some of his seamen and soldiers and rowed ashore in the longboat. Very quickly he was to learn that the Florida Indians were a different breed from the docile and passive Taino Indians encountered in the islands.

As soon as the longboat hit the beach the Indians attacked, trying to seize the boat, the oars, and the weapons of the soldiers. Here we have an insight into the character of Ponce de León which shows that he was not one of the bloodthirsty "treat 'em rough" school like Cortés, De Soto, and others. He had instructed his men not to provoke the Indians and to try and seek a peaceful encounter. In speaking of this obviously planned and unprovoked attack by the Indians, Herrera says, "in order not to break with them (the Indians), they suffered it, not wanting to cause trouble in the land. But because they struck a seaman in the head with a club, from which he remained unconscious, they had to fight with them; they, with their arrows and armed shafts—the points of sharpened bones and fish spines—wounded two Spaniards, and the Indians received little hurt."

After this less than satisfactory episode, Ponce de León pulled anchor and moved to a nearby stream (Jupiter Inlet) to take on firewood and water while awaiting the return of the bergantina. These Florida Indians apparently considered the Spaniards as uninvited and unwelcome intruders (come to think of it, that's what they were) and a war party of sixty attacked while the Spaniards were gathering their firewood and water. In this skirmish, Ponce de León captured one Indian for use as a guide. These Indians never volunteered for guide duty, so we find all the early explorers from Columbus on had to capture them and impress them into the job.

Ponce de León stayed at Jupiter Inlet for some time awaiting the return of the errant bergantina. While there he placed on the shore an inscribed stone cross and named the river, "La Cruz." That cross has never been found but, as might be expected, phonies occasionally make their appearance.

On 8 May with the bergantina back in place and enough wind to fight the current Ponce de León finally rounded "Cabo de los Corrientes" and anchored at a village named Abaioa which would be located near Lake Worth Inlet. He didn't go ashore here so he must have learned the name of the village from his new Indian guide.

Figure 16. The "Santiago" at anchor near the shores of Florida.

The "Cabo de los Corrientes" which they rounded can be quite positively identified as the Cape just north of Lake Worth Inlet, but Herrera has muddied the water here by inserting his own interpretation. He said that they were rounding the "Cape of La Florida" which was on maps of his time (usually at Biscayne Bay). In reality they were still north of that point.

The log entry then continues, "all this coast, from Punta de Arracifes, to Cabo de los Corrientes, runs north by northwest and south by southeast and is clean, and of a depth of 6 brazas and the cape lies in 28 degrees, 15 minutes (latitude)." The coast to "Cabo de los Corrientes" does run north by northwest and south by southeast and is clean, but where is "Punta de Arracifes"? Ponce de León hasn't mentioned this landmark before. This is obviously another insertion by Herrera from a later map and should be disregarded; he may have located it incorrectly as he did the Cape of La Florida.

Alaminos reports "Cabo de los Corrientes" at 28 degrees, 15 minutes, latitude while it is actually at 26 degrees, 48 minutes. Alaminos has now shortened his northerly error to one degree, 27 minutes and that is certainly understandable since his dead reckoning calculations were based upon his estimate of speed and distance from fifteen different short, slow moving legs in unknown currents.

Ponce de León continued sailing south and at this point the log reads,

". . . they navigated until they found two islands to the south in 27 degrees, to one which had a league of unimpaired shoreline, they assigned the name Santa Marta, they took on water at her." Santa Marta is Key Biscayne, which has a little over a Spanish league (3½ miles) of unimpaired shoreline and the other island is Virginia Key. These are the first two islands south of Lake Worth Inlet (Cabo de los Corrientes).

Alaminos reports the latitude of Santa Marta (Key Biscayne) at 27 degrees when it actually lies at 25 degrees, 42 minutes, which indicates that he is now calculating his latitude one degree, 18 minutes too far north. His last two latitudes have not been as consistent as the others. I can only suggest that he is not able accurately to estimate these strong and changing currents in his calculations. Another factor is that on this southerly course the variation factor would be different than it was on the northwesterly course.

The next entry reads, "Friday 13 May, they made sail, running along the edge of a sandbank, and reef of islands, as far as an island they call Pola, which lies in 26 degrees, 30 minutes, and between the shoal and the reef of islands, and the mainland it extends toward the great sea like a bay." Pola is most probably Key Largo and Ponce de León was running down Hawk Channel between the outer reef and the Keys. Even with a modern chart and ample channel markers this passage is still tricky for a deep draft sailboat so I have to admire the ability and seamanship of these Spanish sailors in negotiating this channel without a problem. Herrera's remark about the mainland and about Florida Bay extending to the Gulf of Mexico (the great sea) is an insertion based upon his later knowledge which would, of course, have been unknown to Ponce de León. The latitude here is meaningless since Key Largo is such a long island extending north-northeast and south-southwest that the latitude could vary by over 1/2 a degree depending upon the spot from which it was measured.

Starting here, the log is vague as to specific islands but it is apparent that Ponce de León continued down Hawk Channel to within sight of the Tortugas, naming the string of keys or islands "Los Mártires." Alaminos reports that the Keys (Los Mártires) lie at latitude 26 degrees, 15 minutes while Key West and the adjacent keys actually lie at 24 degrees, 35 minutes so his northerly error now becomes one degree, 40 minutes, about the midpoint or average of the range of his northerly errors.

Ponce de León said he named the string of islands "Los Mártires" (the martyrs) because, at a distance as they came into view, they appeared like men who were suffering. I've looked at the Keys from a distance many times and I must admit I can't quite see those suffering men. However, at a later date this name was to prove most appropriate, as many a shipwrecked sailor cast ashore in the Keys was promptly murdered by the bellicose and unfriendly Calusa Indians.

From Key West Ponce de León sailed west past the Marquesas Keys, then leaving the Tortugas to port, turned north and east to explore the backside of this island of La Florida that he had discovered. At this point the sailing directions are so vague, saying only that he sailed "sometimes to the north, and at others to the northeast," that it is quite useless to try and plot or re-sail his track. But we can easily pinpoint the landfall and subsequent anchorage from the geographical description of the coast in the log. It is from this anchorage on the west coast of Florida that Ponce de León will make his next significant discovery of a protected deep water harbor which will have a vital impact on the subsequent Spanish exploration of the mainland.

After landfall on 23 May, Herrera's drastically abbreviated summary of the log reads, " . . . and on the 24th they ran along the coast, to the south (not caring to see what was mainland) as far as some islets, which were running out to sea, and because it seemed there was an entrance, between them, and the coast, for the ships, in order to take on water and firewood, they stayed there until 3 June, and careened one ship." This exploration period is shown in Figure 17.

The obvious landfall on 23 May is on the west coast of Florida just north of Gasparilla Island where they turned and sailed south past the islands of La Costa, Captiva, and Sanibel to the wide and deep entrance to San Carlos Bay at the mouth of the Caloosahatchee River. This landfall fits the north and the northeasterly sailing directions and conforms to the geographical description of the islands "running out to sea." The subsequent anchorages have been deduced from a careful study of Ponce de León's reported actions, and from relating these actions to the marine geography of the area to include later knowledge establishing the location of the local Indian village sites.

Ponce de León's first anchorage where he took on firewood and water was off the southeast tip of Sanibel Island, as shown in the chart in Figure 17. He stayed in this vicinity for nine days provisioning the ships and careened one of the ships on the protected bayside beach of Sanibel or on one of the nearby small sand islands. It was here that he was to encounter the wily and belligerent Calusa Indians and their crafty cacique (king) named Carlos.

The Calusa Indians, more than any other Florida tribe, had a tremendous and telling impact on the history of early Spanish exploration and conquest of Florida. This vital fact has been overlooked or treated summarily by previous historians. The history of Spain's attempt at subjugating these unconquerable peoples, first under Ponce de León in 1521, then by later Spanish efforts will be covered in Chapter 5. For now we will only examine Ponce de León's brief first encounter with the indomitable Calusa in his 1513 voyage.

While at anchor off Sanibel, the Indians first sent several canoes to reconnoiter the Spaniards but they made no contact. Then the Indians beckoned from shore that the Spaniards should land, but Ponce de León, probably made wary of that seemingly friendly gesture by his encounter on the east coast, decided to remain on the boats. Then when one of the Spanish boats raised an anchor to repair it, the Indians thought they were leaving, so they went into action. Several canoes came

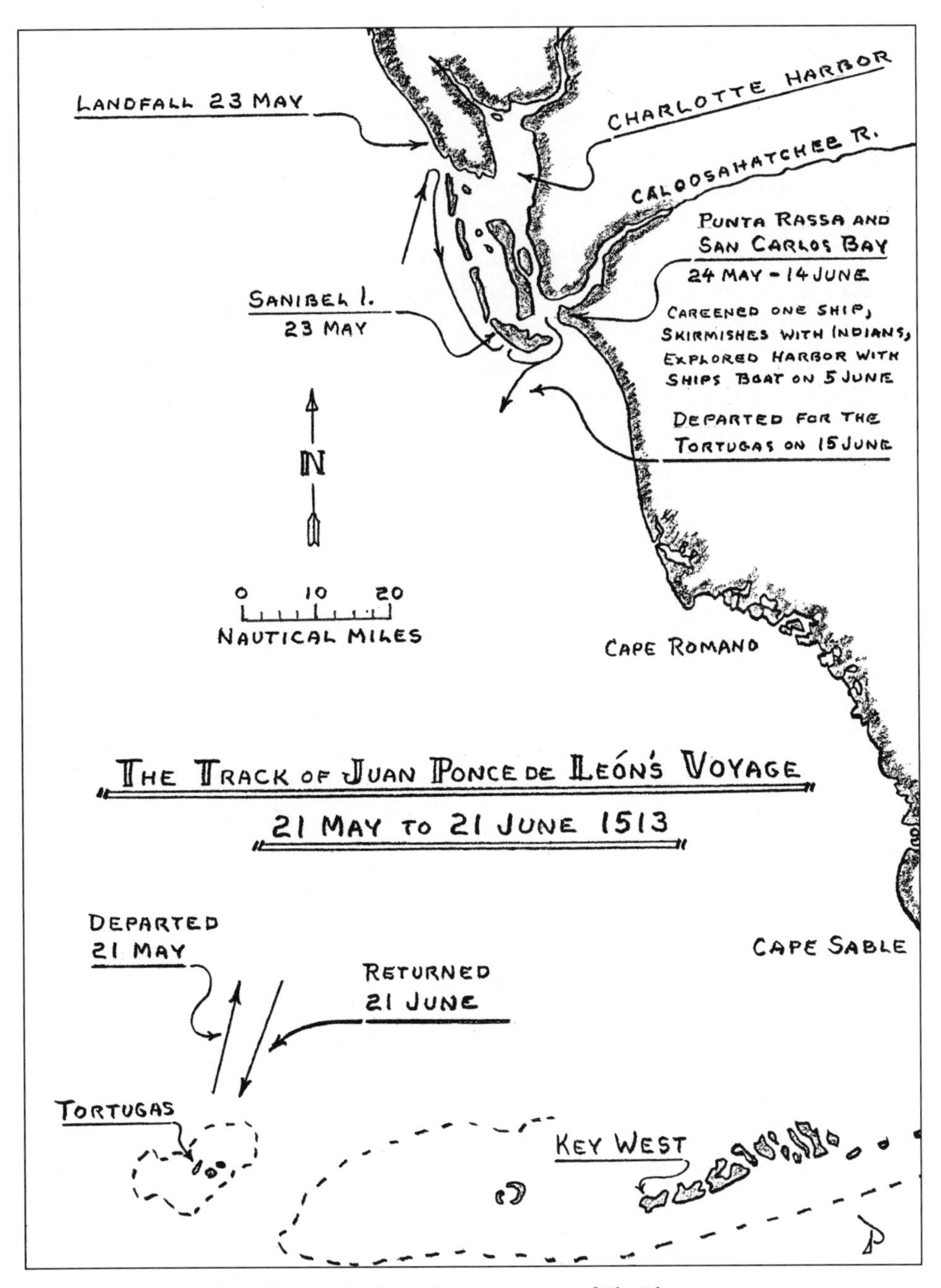

Figure 17. Ponce de León's track along the west coast of Florida.

out from shore and, grabbing the anchor, tried to tow the ship ashore. Ponce de León then sent the armed longboat into action and the Spaniards chased the Indians back to shore without a fight.

Then what did the Spaniards in the longboat do? They went ashore, captured four women and brought them back to the boats! What have we here? Ponce de León has just broken another precedent.

All other early Spanish explorers had captured only male warriors to use as guides or hold for ransom in negotiation. Women were of no use for this, so why did the longboat bring back four women? Again I am going to suggest the overwhelmingly obvious answer. Ponce de León's men were simply tired of watching him and Ortega sporting around with their women, while they were forced to live a celibate life, so they decided to do something about it! And they probably did it with Ponce de León's approval or even suggestion, because any good military commander knows it's important to keep the troops happy. I might make the observation that it would seem that Ponce de León's men didn't need that fountain of youth any more than he did.

After this incident involving the kidnapping of the women, there were several days during which the Indians were subdued and peaceful and the Spaniards were able to trade with them for skins and guanin, a poor grade of gold with a high copper content. Ponce de León learned at this time that the Calusa king named Carlos lived across the bay and was reputed to have plenty of gold, so he prepared to move his anchorage from Sanibel closer to this king with the gold. But before he could get underway an Indian who spoke Spanish (Herrera suggests that he was an escaped slave from Española) came out in a canoe and told him to wait where he was as Carlos would come the next day with gold to trade.

This must have seemed almost too good to be true and indeed that's exactly what it proved to be. Carlos came the next day right on time, but not with gold. He came in a cunning and carefully planned attack with twenty canoes, some fastened together in pairs, and sent his warriors in the battle, some to attack the ships while others tried to cut the anchor cables. But the Spaniards with their superior firepower prevailed, killing a number of Indians, capturing four, while losing only one Spaniard to the Indian arrows.

Notwithstanding this show of deceit and hostility, Ponce de León was still determined to try and cement friendly relations with Carlos, so as a goodwill gesture, he sent two of the captives back with instructions to say that he sought peace with the Indians. Then he followed through on his original plan and on 5 June moved his anchorage across the bay (San Carlos Bay) in order to pursue this hoped-for peaceful contact with Carlos. We will learn later Carlos had his headquarters on Estero Island on the southeast side of San Carlos Bay so that is the area that Ponce de León was seeking in this move.

As chief pilot, Alaminos preceded the ships in the longboat. He sounded the bay to select the best anchorage site and no doubt made a chart of the harbor for future use, in keeping with his duties as chief pilot. During this reconnoiter Alaminos would have discovered that the wide deep mouth of the Caloosahatchee River, where it empties into San Carlos Bay, could accommodate many deep draft vessels at a time. On the south side of the river at what is now Punta Rassa he would have found a deep spot right at the shore where vessels could tie up as at a wharf. But for protection against the Indian attacks, Ponce de León would want to anchor offshore beyond the range of arrows. Thus his most probable site for this second anchorage is at the north end of Estero Island in about fourteen feet of water where the holding is good. Charlotte Harbor has been proposed as the harbor they explored and in which they anchored. However, Charlotte Harbor is a large and shallow, almost landlocked, inland bay with only a tortuous, winding, dredged entrance through nearly three miles of offshore shoals, which hardly deserves the name of harbor.

I have given Ponce de León's postulated anchorage at this spot in a rather definitive manner even giving the depth of water and holding properties of the bottom. Am I sure of this information? Positively! I anchored in this spot for four days in early June which is the time of the year that Ponce de León was here and for about the same amount of time. I didn't see any Indians with their log canoes, only noisy outboards scattering empty beer cans and plastic cups. I think I would rather have the Indians.

At this second anchorage the Indians pulled the same crafty stunt they pulled before and apparently Ponce de León fell for it. The Indians said that the Spaniards should not depart because the next day Carlos was going to come with gold to trade. Carlos did come the next day, but again, not with gold but with eighty armed canoes. This time the engagement took on somewhat the aspect of a sham battle. The Indians, learning from their first battle, stayed just out of range of the crossbows and artillery. Their arrows fell harmlessly into the sea short of the ships.

Carlos with his large flotilla of war canoes must have been more of a seafaring naval power (relatively speaking) than is usually described. Very little is known of these large Indian war canoes as none of them have survived intact. These canoes were made from hollowed out logs and the larger canoes could accommodate up to forty people. The larger canoes indicate that the Calusa and other Florida Indians along the Gulf coast made seafaring excursions to the islands and to Mexico just as the Taino Indians did. Recent archaeological digs in the vicinity of Fort Walton Beach have shown that the larger canoes were made from large tropical trees native to the rain forests of Mexico or Central America and not found in Florida. This same dig uncovered a ball of copal incense which could only have come from the tropical forests of Central America where the Maya harvested and processed the incense.

Indian artifacts from the archaeological site on Mound Key in the vicinity of the village of Carlos indicate Maya or Mexican origin. Thus it is quite likely that Carlos' aggressive attacks on the Spaniards could have resulted largely from a desire to obtain these large seafaring vessels for his own use in seafaring trade between Florida and the Yucatan. A sixteenth century depiction of one of the smaller canoes is pictured in Figure 18.

Figure 18. Indian log canoe.

Ponce de León finally decided he couldn't do business with this obstinate Carlos so he departed on 14 April, stopping at Sanibel to take on more water and naming the island "Matanca" (killing), for the Indians and the Spaniard killed there. Ponce de León probably felt that his stay in San Carlos Bay had been a dismal failure, but such is not the case. By discovering the large deep water harbor in San Carlos Bay and having Alaminos make a chart of it, Ponce de León had made another significant discovery which was to have a profound impact on future Spanish exploration of the mainland.

The first Spanish explorer to utilize this harbor was Hernández de Córdoba who used it as a harbor of refuge in 1517 when returning to Cuba from his unplanned discovery of the Yucatan. In his encounter with Indian warriors, Córdoba lost one of his three ships and nearly half of his complement of soldiers and sailors and was badly in need of water. His chief pilot was Alaminos who knew that, with the prevailing winds and currents, the closest harbor of refuge with adequate water was in the Bay of Carlos on La Florida, so he laid a course for that destination.

Arriving in the bay, Alaminos cautioned Córdoba that the Indians here would give fight so twenty soldiers were sent ashore with Alaminos and the water barrels. They did indeed run into a fight and here once again the Indians were intent on seizing the boats rather than just fighting off the intruders. Before the fight was over, the Spaniards had lost one man and had half a dozen more wounded including Alaminos, but they did get their needed water and continued on to Cuba.

Following Córdoba, Alonzo Alvarez de Pineda appeared on the scene in 1519 with Alaminos as chief pilot. Pineda met with the same hostile reception as had Ponce de León and Córdoba earlier and wisely decided not to stay and fight it out even though he had a large military force on board. He then continued on, following the coast, and discovered the Mississippi River before he explored the coast as far as Texas. Spanish pilots were ordered to keep their charts secret from the Portuguese, French, and English but by now the Alaminos chart would be common knowledge to other Spanish pilots who would use the harbor in later explorations.

The next European activity in the harbor was in 1527 when a vessel arrived carrying supplies from Cuba to Pánfilo Narváez who was exploring the coast north of the Tampa Bay area. The captain of the supply vessel was unsure where Narváez was located so he sent four men ashore at San Carlos Bay to see if they could find him. This was a mistake as the Calusa Indians quickly captured them and hauled them away.

I have concluded that the next explorer to utilize the harbor was Hernando de Soto in 1539, but this is a decidedly controversial point. In 1939 a blue-ribbon commission composed of many leading historians was given the task of determining the landing place of De Soto and also his subsequent track through the several southeastern states. In their voluminous final report, the commission determined that De Soto landed on the south side of the Manatee River in lower Tampa Bay. This commission report was then seemingly set in concrete when the U. S. Park Service installed a park and monument at Shaw's Point on the south side of the Manatee River, commemorating that place as the historic landing site.

The findings of the official commission went uncontested for over two decades until Warren H. Wilkinson, a respected Florida historian, wrote a paper in which he attacked the findings of the commission as flawed and stated that the evidence pointed to a landing further south in the Fort Myers area. This was followed in 1968 by a comprehensive and thoroughly documented study by Rolfe F. Schell which supported a landing at the mouth of the Caloosahatchee River near Fort Myers Beach. The Schell book contained a detailed analysis of the reports of the four separate chroniclers of the expedition to support this landing site. His thesis was supported with accurate charts and a lucid explanation to show the daily progress of the vessels into the bay and river and then the inland track from Fort Myers (Ucita) to Tallahassee (Apalachee).

I have not gone deeply into this subject and base my conclusion solely on the navigation involved in the landing site. Before leaving Cuba with nine heavily loaded ships, De Soto wisely sent out the experienced Spanish pilot Juan de Añasco to search for a suitable landing site. Añasco would certainly have known of Alaminos' charted harbor in San Carlos Bay and would seek it for the landing site. Upon his return to Cuba, Añasco reported he had found a good harbor seventy-five or eighty leagues north of Havana. Both the distance and the compass heading fit San Carlos Bay and not Tampa Bay. The logistics of landing this large expeditionary force, including 570 heavily armed men and equipment and 223 horses, would further point to the deep wharf-like spot on the south side of the Caloosahatchee River at Punta Rassa rather than the south side of the shallow, inaccessible Manatee River in lower Tampa Bay.

Leaving San Carlos Bay on 14 June, Ponce de León headed back south to the Keys which he had left in May to explore the western shore of his La Florida. He headed for the last of the Keys (Tortugas) which he had seen to the west just before he turned north to San Carlos Bay, and arrived there on 21 June. Here he was able to provision his ships with fresh meat, taking 160 of the loggerhead turtles that nested there. Then appropriately enough, he named this group of islands the Tortugas, a name which has survived and is on present day charts. This nesting colony of loggerhead turtles has long since been depleted, but there is now a heroic effort underway to re-establish the nesting grounds on Loggerhead Key in the Tortugas. It is interesting to note here that they also captured fourteen "sea wolves" which is the Spanish term for a seal. The present seal species are limited to cold water and seldom are seen south of Cape Cod. So these must have been a warm water species that were wiped out in colonial times.

Now we come to an interesting and somewhat perplexing change of plans. When departing the Tortugas on 24 June, Ponce de León decided to sail on a course of southwest by west. At this point we must question why he abandoned his search to the north and selected the precise course of southwest by west. All of his other courses across unknown waters in search of Beniny were to the north, so why did he now sail such a finite course and in a direction that is contrary to his fixation that Beniny lay somewhere north of the Lucayans?

I can only conclude the Indians must have finally convinced Ponce de León that the rich land with much gold which he was seeking was not to the north. They pointed southwest by west, straight to the Yucatan. The two new Indian guides he picked up in San Carlos Bay may have been a factor in this change of course. In describing how the Indians pointed to the Yucatan, I would remind the reader how I have shown previously that there is evidence of Indian trade between Florida and the Yucatan.

Now's his chance! He is finally on the right track to find that wealthy new land, with mountains full of gold, large cities with paved streets, houses and temples of stone that rival the pyramids, and an exotic and advanced civilization rather than these wretched naked Indians. That is just what he had in mind. All of that is in the Yucatan and he is headed right for it on this southwest by west course with three well provisioned ships. But does he get there? Sadly he doesn't, and my sailed duplication of his voyage from the Tortugas toward the Yucatan will show you why.

This leg from the Tortugas is critical to determine exactly where he landed after sailing this new course for 2½ days. Also this is one of the legs where my use of a sailing vessel to arrive at the true track over the bottom cannot help but be better than attempting to plot the track using non-empirical estimates for the influence of the currents.

The southwest by west heading is 236 degrees on my compass and when corrected for the Seville compass error and the two degrees easterly magnetic variation which prevailed in the area in 1513, my true heading to be sailed becomes 233 degrees to duplicate Ponce de León's track. I sailed on this heading at a speed of 2.6 knots through the water, which I had determined by computation of the time and distance of previous legs was his average speed with favorable wind conditions. Ponce de León may have sailed at a reduced speed at night and faster during the day, but this would produce only a slight "S" curve variance in the track ending up at the same place. My sailed and recorded track, sailed on the same (corrected) compass heading, at the same speed, through the same waters and currents, thus becoming the true track, accurately shows where Ponce de León made landfall on a shoreline which he could not identify.

My recorded track over the bottom is illustrated in Figure 19. I recorded a Sat-Nav and a Loran-C (computerized electronic navigation instruments) fix every four hours. These sophisticated electronic navigation instruments using both shore stations and satellites can pinpoint my position within a few hundred feet as well as give me an accurate speed over the bottom and an accurate drift reading in tenths of a degree. The fixes are numbered for convenience in analysis. You will notice the loop current from the northwest began almost immediately pushing my vessel (like the Spanish vessels) south of the sailed heading. In fixes 7 through 11, I have reached the axis of the Gulf Stream (technically the "Florida Current" but by popular usage the "Gulf Stream"). The track is actually pushed back east and the four hour distance over the bottom cut nearly in half. Beginning at fix 11 and through fix 13, the current diminishes and the course picks up a more westerly vector and the speed and distance over the bottom increase. I terminated my sailed track twelve miles from the coast of Cuba as I am required to do by State Department regulations.

A look at the track in Figure 19 through currents which are constantly changing in both speed and direction should convince anyone with even a rudimentary knowledge of navigation that it would be virtually impossible to program these currents into a computer. This proves that my use of a sailing vessel to duplicate the track is the superior method. I determined that Ponce de León's track would have ended 58 nautical miles west of Havana just west of a harbor at Bahia Honda and on the 10 fathom shelf where there would be ample anchorage sites for his brief exploration of the coast. They saw signs of habitation, but no Indians. At this point they could not decide whether this was some new unknown land or Cuba. The only geographical description they gave was that the coast ran east-west which would fit the coast of both Cuba and the Yucatan. While the extreme eastern end of Cuba was occupied by the Spanish at this time, the central portion and western end were unknown and unexplored wilderness so it is no small wonder that Ponce de León could not identify the coast.

They do mention Cuba, but only with a confusing and ambiguous statement that "they found themselves 18 full leagues abaft the beam for it to be Cuba." This is Kelley's translation. Spofford translates this as "off course" which is equally

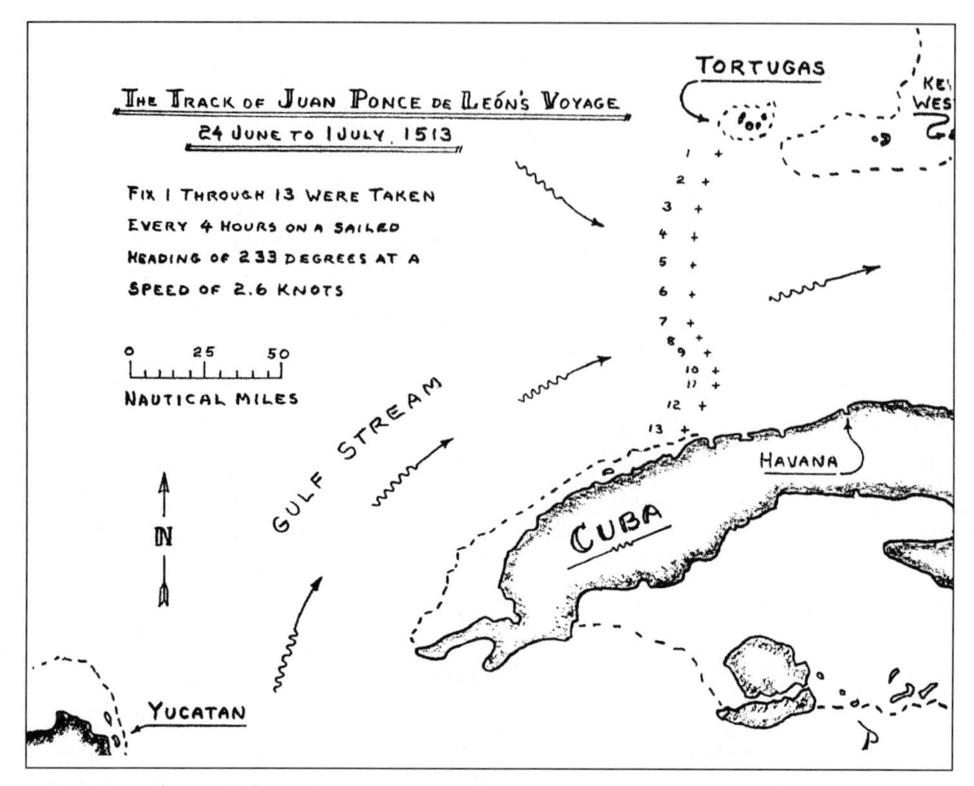

Figure 19. The track from the Tortugas to Cuba.

ambiguous. Does this mean it is not Cuba because it is located 18 leagues (about 54 nautical miles) in the wrong direction? This seems a small error in view of their extensive voyage away from any known landmark. We will probably never know what they meant by that remark and esoteric conjecture about it serves no useful purpose.

There are prominent historians who contend that Ponce de León did in fact reach the Yucatan on this leg and so became the discoverer of Mexico. Now most history books and encyclopedias carry this as fact. The most prominent of these historians are Samuel Eliot Morison in his book *The European Discovery of America: The Southern Voyages* (1974), and Aurelio Tío in his paper "Historia del descubrimiento de la Florida y Bimeni o Yucatan" (1972). Both authors base their opinion on depositions in court records made many years later when petitioners (probably Ponce de León's surviving relatives) tried to establish land grants in the Yucatan. This is hardly a valid source to establish a historical landfall when we have a copy of the navigator's log which proves otherwise.

An attempt by Diego Columbus in 1519 to kill the claims of Cortés and Velasquez to the newly discovered Yucatan resulted in one more spurious sixteenth century document which seemed to tie the Yucatan to the Ponce de León voyage. To establish his claim to the newly discovered land Diego petitioned the crown and asserted, "these lands now called Ulloa Yucatan, were formally called Beimeni (Beniny) among Christians." These "Christians" referred to are the colonists in the Indies under the jurisdiction of Diego so it was by this vague legal technicality that he hoped to establish his claim to the Yucatan as part of the Indies rather than as a new undiscovered land. I have shown earlier that the Indians were trying to tell Ponce de León that the fabulous and wealthy Beniny which he sought was on the Yucatan but he couldn't understand them and persisted in his belief that it was an island in the northern Lucayans. Now we have Diego Columbus confirming that fact by quoting from unknown Indian sources who told him (and his "Christians") the same thing. Diego's report does indeed tie the name Beimeni (Beniny) to the Yucatan, but it cannot be construed as showing that Ponce de León's voyage touched there.

Those who argue that Ponce de León landed in the Yucatan should consider these hard, cold, mathematical facts: to reach the Yucatan from the Tortugas in 2½ days Ponce de León would have to sail at a speed of 6.75 knots to make the 300 miles against an average current of 1.5 knots. This speed is not only quite unattainable for their vessels, but rather than the southwest by west heading (236 degrees) reported in the log, he would be forced to sail a heading of 260 degrees for the first half of the leg to avoid being swept down to Cuba. Then, about halfway, he would have to change to a heading of 205 degrees to make the Yucatan. This is a highly unlikely (and unbelievable) scenario and completely at odds with the log.

After briefly exploring this unidentified shoreline, Ponce de León no doubt decided it wasn't the wealthy and grand island of Beniny which he sought. Probably running short of both patience and provisions he left Cuba on the first of July for the return to Puerto Rico. He elected to retrace his path through the northern Lucayans because he was sure that Beniny was to be found there. As a last desperate effort before leaving the Lucayans, he sent one ship with Juan Perez de Ortubio as Captain and Antón de Alaminos as pilot to search once more the northern Lucayans for Beniny. I have made no attempt to re-trace this portion of the voyage in a definitive manner as it does not contribute to identifying his discovery landfalls.

Ponce de León reached Puerto Rico about the middle of October without ever finding his sought after Beniny. Ortubio and Alaminos returned a short time later after finding a large wooded island (probably Andros). They proudly announced that it was Beniny, even though everyone must have known it was just one more of the primitive windswept Lucayan islands inhabited by a few of the remaining poor and frightened Taino Indians.

We can forgive Ortubio and Alaminos for saying they had found the island of Beniny even though they knew it wasn't true. After all, their boss had told them to go find that damn island which he thought was out there somewhere, so what else could they do but say "we found it." Ponce de León obviously didn't believe they had found his grand and wealthy island of Beniny because at a later date he only laid claim to the new island of La Florida and petitioned the King to allow him to found a colony there.

But the fact that Ortubio and Alaminos reported that Beniny was in the northwest part of the Lucayans resulted in cartographers in the sixteenth and seventeenth century placing an island by that name on their charts. In later charts and maps of the area the island of Beniny, with several changes in spelling, migrated around in the same general area and eventually became the small island of Bimini in the Bahamas across the Gulf Stream east of Miami.

Some historians still go to great pains examining sixteenth and seventeenth century cartography trying to pin down just which island is the alleged Beniny found by Alaminos, but who cares? The island never existed! The numerous Indian guides on the explorers' ships never pointed to it and said "that's Beniny," because they never knew it as an island. Regardless of the name involved, when asked about a grand and wealthy island or a land located to the north, the Indians would have told about the Yucatan and not the Lucayans. Those obstinate Spaniards just couldn't understand this so they searched for the wrong thing in the wrong place.

Thus ends the story of the fruitless search for the elusive island of Beniny. However, Ponce de León was determined to salvage something from this exploration venture so he elected to return to La Florida at a later date and establish a colony which he hoped would prosper.

4

The Return to La Florida and Death

Following his exploration voyage, Ponce de León returned to Spain in 1514 to report on the voyage and lay claim to the newly discovered island of La Florida. Very little is known of his activities for six years following this visit since his actions would not require the keeping and submission of a detailed log as was the case of his exploration voyage.

We do know that Ferdinand conferred on Ponce de León the title of "Adelantado" or governor of the island of La Florida and authorized him to establish a permanent settlement at a place of his own choosing. But Ferdinand granted this concession with a proviso that Ponce de León was first to lead a military expeditionary campaign against the Caribs in the islands east and south of Puerto Rico, after which he could use the ships and soldiers to conquer and settle La Florida.

The Caribs, who had been harassing the new Spanish settlers in the islands, were scattered over more than one thousand miles of the lesser Antilles so this was no small task which Ferdinand had given to Ponce de León. Although we know very little of the details of this campaign we can say it was successful since the Caribs were eliminated as a threat. And we can also say that the campaign must have taken the better part of six years since Ponce de León did not apply to use the ships and the military force in his settlement of La Florida until 1521.

In February, 1521, Ponce de León wrote to Emperor Charles V (who succeeded Ferdinand) indicating his intention to return to La Florida with a number of people to found and settle a colony. In this letter he also said he intended to explore the shore further and see whether it was an island or if it was the mainland joined to the land of "Nueva España" (Mexico) recently conquered by Cortés. He did not live to make that exploration. This is indeed sad because if he had he would have realized that he had made a momentous discovery rather than just finding another unimportant island.

He sailed from Puerto Rico on 26 February 1521 in two ships loaded with settlers and supporting gear necessary to establish a permanent Spanish town and fort on the shores of La Florida. The settlers included farmers with their cattle, sheep and swine, and seeds and young plants to make the colony self supporting for food. Then there were journeymen from all the trades, soldiers with their horses and dogs to subdue the Indians, and finally priests to minister to the colonists and friars to convert and establish missions for the Indians.

We have a record of what was aboard his ships, but no record of where he intended to land and establish this colony. However, here we can use a bit of logic and easily find the answer. The early Spanish colonizers had three main requirements in selecting the site of a new colony. These were, (a) adjacent to a good deep water port for the ships, (b) an ample source of good drinking water, and (c) the geography of the area must lend itself to a good perimeter defense against a hostile force.

Ponce de León had met all three of these requirements in Sanibel Island (Matanca), so it is the only logical site for his colony. He also had Alaminos' chart and personal knowledge of the harbor as he had previously anchored and obtained good water there for his ships. The Island was also close enough to the mainland for easy access, yet would provide a perfect perimeter defense against hostile Indians.

All of this sounds perfect but Ponce de León unknowingly made a grave error in selecting Sanibel as the site of his future colony and town. He underestimated the tenacious fighting ability of the Calusa Indians and he overestimated his ability to bring about a peaceful coexistence with Carlos, the Calusa cacique, through either negotiation or military force. In this we must remember that Ponce de León had spent most of his adult life fighting the Taino and Carib Indians and had always been able to prevail, but these Calusa Indians were quite determined to prevent any encroachment on their territory by the Spaniards.

The settlers were fiercely attacked from the moment they landed. They were attacked while they were erecting their buildings, and attacked when they attempted to plant their crops and tend their cattle. Many settlers died from the incessant attacks. Others died from illness brought on from being forced to live huddled together in the compound in unhealthy conditions, afraid to venture forth for fear of being attacked. Ponce de León tried to stick it out for a few months but finally, after receiving a painful wound in the thigh, decided to abandon the project and withdrew the company to the safety of Cuba.

Ponce de León died from his festered wound in Puerto Principe, Cuba in July 1521, at the age of 47. He must have died exceedingly frustrated and disappointed. He failed in his quest to find the wealthy island of Beniny and then failed in his dream of establishing a colony from which he could govern his newly discovered island of La Florida. It is sad indeed that Ponce de León died without realizing that his momentous discovery of the mainland, of the Gulf Stream, and the first deep water harbor on the mainland were to have a profound effect on the development of Spanish conquest in the New World.

Juan Ponce de León was first buried in Puerto Principe, Cuba where he died. Later in the century his remains were removed to San Juan de Puerto Rico where they now rest in the cathedral of San Juan. Juan Ponce de León's epitaph reads:

Mole sub hac fortis requiescunt ossa Leónis
Qui vivit factis nomina magna suis.

Beneath this structure rest the bones of a Lion
Who performed deeds mightier than his name.

The story of Ponce de León's discovery of Florida would seem to end in a discordant note with his death. But does the story really end there? Indeed it doesn't, and Chapter 5 provides a fitting conclusion to the true and complete story.

5

The Spanish Encounter The Calusa Indians

We cannot close the history of the failed attempts at colonization of southwest Florida beginning with Ponce de Léon without examining the true cause for this failure. Historians have been quick to lay the blame for Ponce de Léon's failure on his alleged mistreatment of the Indians, but this is far from the truth. We have seen in Ponce de León's previous encounters with the Florida Indians how he continually sought peace, instructing his men not to provoke the Indians and to fight only when lives were in danger.

Ponce de León's colony in Florida was doomed to fail because of the indomitable spirit and character of the Calusa Indians and their leaders.

The Calusa Indians were unique among all the varied tribes of Florida in that they were never conquered or subdued by the Spanish. They were a powerful fisher-hunter-gatherer society with a complex political and military order normally found only among the settled Indians who raised crops. The name of the tribe derived from Calus, the name of their principal town or province as well as the name of their cacique or chief. Ponce de León was the first to convert the cacique's name from the Indian Calus to the Spanish equivalent Carlos, so from that time on we find the caciques of the Calusa tribe were called Carlos. It is significant that the Spanish, in referring to the leaders of other tribes always called them caciques or chiefs, but referred to Carlos as king.

In their complex social and political system the Calusa had different grades of nobles and military and religious leaders. They demanded and received tribute from neighboring tribes who were required to cement the treaty by sending one of their chief's daughters as a wife for Carlos. This polygamy was reserved for Carlos alone as a matter of state as all other Calusa were monogamous.

Carlos had his headquarters and principal village sites in the Fort Myers area but the tribe was a large one scattered in more than thirty villages over much of southwest Florida. The Calusa domain, including tributary tribal areas, was roughly all of south Florida including the Keys, south of a line drawn across the State from a point

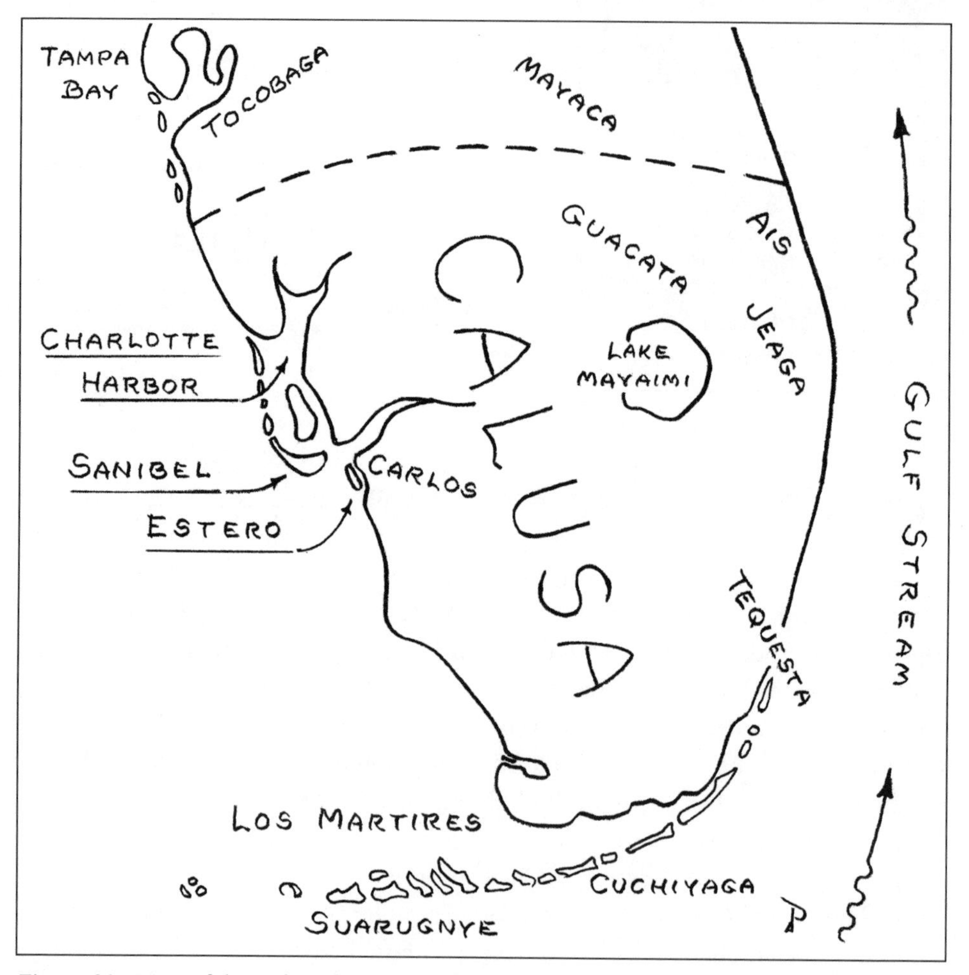

Figure 20. Map of the Calusa domain in Florida.

north of Charlotte Harbor, then north of Lake Okeechobee, thence to the east coast in the vicinity of Stuart and the St. Lucie Inlet.

Fontaneda tells us that the tributary tribes in Carlos' domain included the Guacata in central Florida, the Ais, Jeaga, and Tequesta on the east coast, and the Suarugnye and Cuchiyaga in the Keys. From this we can see that Carlos would have been informed of Ponce de León's expedition well before he arrived in San Carlos Bay on the west coast of Florida.

Carlos was the supreme ruler in all matters of state. His second in command (usually a brother or cousin) was a military leader called the "Great Captain." At scheduled intervals Carlos would hold court, seated on a wicker throne on a raised platform in much the same manner as kings have done down through the ages.

Their religious beliefs encompassed one supreme God who created the earth and the cosmos and all the creatures therein. The cosmos and the fate of all mankind were governed by three beings with the one supreme God being paramount. This religious concept gave the Spanish missionaries a problem because, in explaining the Trinity, the Indians thought they were just teaching them a part of their own religion, so probably said, "we already know that."

While the Calusa concept of creation and an afterlife was similar to Judeo-Christian traditions, the remainder of their religion was pagan in every respect. They believed in an afterlife and buried their dead ancestors in holy places with priests performing a religious ritual, a procedure which is comparable to those of the Judeo-Christian and related traditions. However, Calusa pagan beliefs came to the fore with their numerous idols represented by large grotesque face masks which the priests and shamans wore during religious rites. But by far the most important and overpowering aspect of this religion was the fanatical devotion of the Calusa, which obviated any proselytizing efforts by the Spanish.

Ponce de León's abortive attempt to found a colony among the Calusa Indians was only the first of several failed attempts by the Spanish. By the middle of the sixteenth century the Spaniards were firmly entrenched in St. Augustine, with satellite missions across northern and central Florida. The missions, led by both Franciscan and Jesuit friars, were very successful in peacefully converting the Indians, first to Catholicism, then to a settled agrarian lifestyle in which they were put to work on the mission plantations. But the missions had stopped short of the Calusa territory because a succession of Kings named Carlos had made it plain to the Spanish that Calusa territory was off limits to the Spanish.

Early in 1566 the governor of Florida, Pedro Menéndez de Aviles, arrived in San Carlos Bay with a large expeditionary force consisting of seven vessels to deal with the recalcitrant Carlos. Menéndez believed that a waterway across Florida existed southwest from the St. Johns' River and emptied into the Gulf near this point, so that could have been the real purpose behind his interest in fortifying the area. Another possible reason might be the hope of finding his son who was aboard a vessel which earlier was lost in a hurricane in the area.

Carlos seemed friendly at first (no doubt due to the large military force facing him), even offering his sister as a wife to cement the relationship. Eager to please, Menéndez promptly married her in a mock ceremony, then made arrangements for a fort and mission to be built on the island where Carlos had his headquarters. I will establish later on that this site was Estero Island in the vicinity of Fort Myers Beach.

Later that year Menéndez sent a body of soldiers and colonists to build and occupy the fort, naming it Fort San Antonio. In the meantime, relations with Carlos had deteriorated and the fort was completed with some difficulty. After less than a year the fort became untenable due to the hostility of the Indians. Accordingly, Menéndez decided to move his forces to a nearby island (probably Sanibel) which afforded better defense against attack. Carlos offered large manned canoes for the move, but luckily Menéndez learned in advance that Carlos had instructed his men to sink the canoes and drown the Spaniards in the deep part of

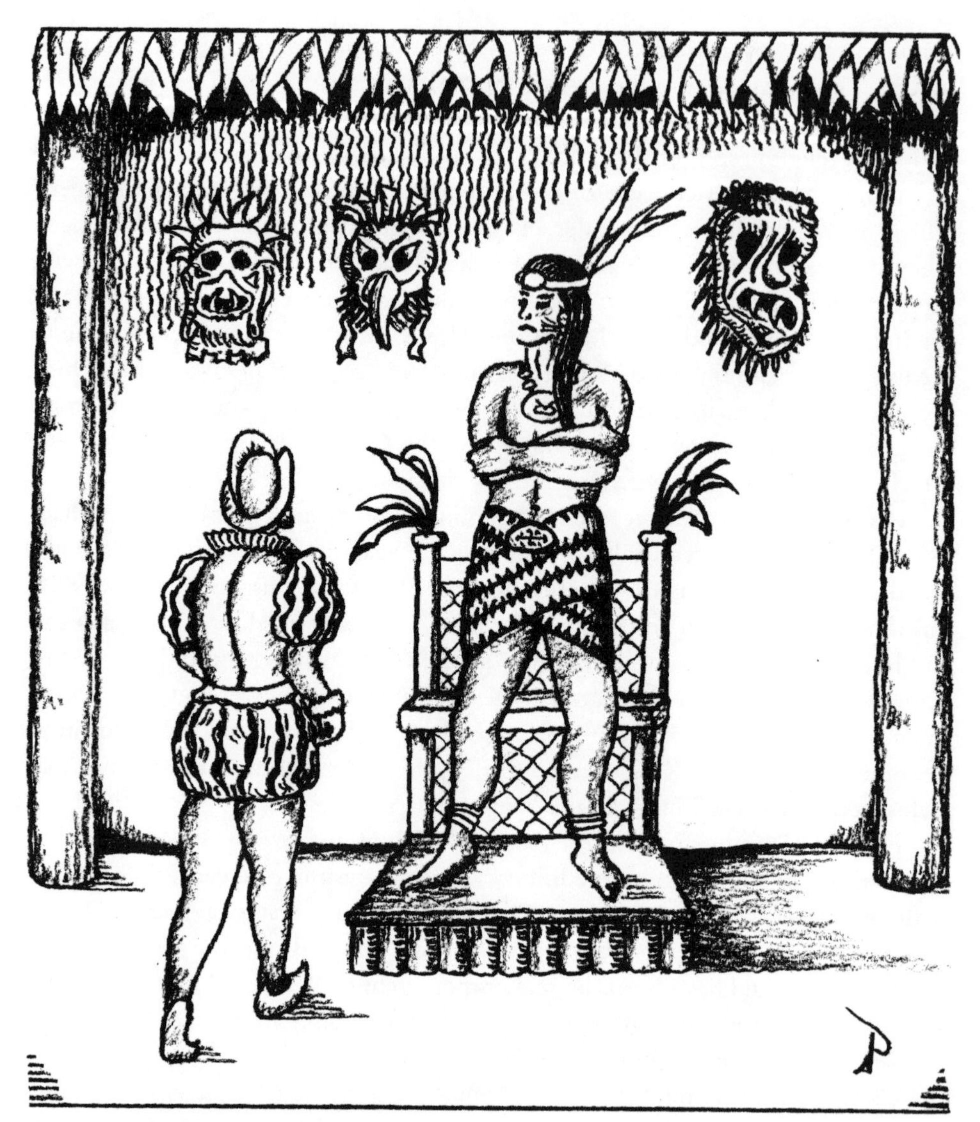

Figure 21. Carlos, King of the Calusa Indians.

the channel. The move was then made with some difficulty using only the ship's launch.

During this later visit Menéndez rescued Hernando de Escalante Fontaneda. We earlier met this young boy who was shipwrecked in the Keys and had lived among the Calusa and neighboring tribes for seventeen years. We can forgive Fontaneda for putting that romantic, false, and fictitious report of the fountain of youth in his memoirs because he also gave us the best first-hand account of the culture, heritage and character of the Calusa Indians. Fontaneda's description of the character of the Calusa can be summed up by his statement that they were a "brave, fierce and skillful people," after which he gave them the dubious honor of being "the meanest people in all of Florida."

It was at this time that the first missionary arrived on the scene. The Jesuit father Juan Rogel had been assigned to start a mission, and to convert Carlos and his people to the Catholic faith. All we can say is, he tried. After nearly a year under constant harassment Father Rogel had not converted or baptized a single Calusa Indian so he gave up and returned to the safety of Cuba. Father Rogel lamented his failure in a long and emotional letter to his superiors, but we should not be too harsh in our judgment of this dedicated Jesuit father as even the Archangel Gabriel would not have succeeded in persuading the Calusa to renounce their religion.

Shortly after Father Rogel departed, Menéndez realized the project would never succeed so he abandoned the fort and withdrew the soldiers and settlers to St. Augustine. After this discouraging event (and probably because of it) the Spanish left the Calusa Indians alone for over a century.

The Governor of Cuba, Pablo de Hita Salazar, launched the final effort to convert Carlos and the Calusa to Catholicism and bring them into the fold of Spanish authority. In September 1697, the Franciscan Fray Feleciano Lopez with five Franciscan brothers embarked for the Bay of Carlos (San Carlos Bay) to once more attempt to establish a mission in Calusa territory. Lopez and his contingent of Franciscan brothers were well equipped with food, clothing, agriculture tools and seed, church furnishings, and assorted trade articles. No soldiers were in this small company as they were intent on peacefully establishing a mission to persuade Carlos and his people to abandon their pagan religion and convert to the Catholic faith. Conversion to the Catholic faith also required the Calusa to abandon their free spirit lifestyle as hunter-fishermen for the quiet life of farmers under the direction of the mission.

To say that Fray Lopez and the Franciscan brothers were in for a rude awakening would be a gross understatement. The master of the transport vessel, fearful of the bellicose nature of the Calusa, anchored well offshore in San Carlos Bay. He stated that the village of Carlos was on a small island about half a league in length and fronting on the Bay. This could only be Estero Island (Fort Myers Beach) as that is the only island fronting on the Bay and approaching that size.

A new young cacique (no doubt also named Carlos) came out to the ship and with two large canoes carried the friars and all their supplies to the village on the island. Once the friars were ashore, the worried master of the transport vessel beat a hasty retreat. Fray Lopez noted that the Calusa lived in sixteen large communal houses and estimated the population of the village to be about 400 people. The friars were housed in a portion of one of the large houses in which they noted, ". . . the roof allowed the sun, the rain, and even the evening dew to come through."

At first the reception of the friars appeared to be friendly. This rapidly changed to hostility, however, when the Indians learned the friars weren't immediately going to start handing out the food and supplies in payment for their vocal acceptance of baptism. The Calusa Indians were fully informed of the operation of the Spanish missions and, upon seeing hoes among the supplies, asked why the friars had not brought their slaves with them since "the Calusa do not know how to use a hoe." In other words, they told the friars they would never abandon their free spirit lifestyle for that of a farmer digging in the ground on a mission plantation.

Fray Lopez and the friars were unmercifully subjected to physical abuse and even threats of death so they quickly realized the futility of their efforts. After only a few weeks Fray Lopez requested some canoes to take them and their supplies to the Keys where they hoped to hail a passing ship. The cacique obliged and furnished several canoes and a complement of Indians to row them on their journey. Then, during the trip to the Keys, the friars were stripped of their remaining supplies, baggage, and even the clothes they wore. They were deposited on Matacumbe Key with no food and wearing only their thin undershirts. After nearly a month, on the verge of starvation, they were picked up by the same vessel that had earlier carried them to the Bay of Carlos.

The location of the home island, the village of Carlos and the Bay of Carlos have been the subject of much poorly informed speculation by historians of this period. I have determined that the Calusa headquarters village of the successive caciques named Carlos was on Estero Island in the vicinity of Fort Myers Beach. The "Bay of Carlos" mentioned in numerous sixteenth century documents is in fact the aptly named San Carlos Bay at the mouth of the Caloosahatchee River. This site for the Bay of Carlos and the Calusa island village differs from that given by most contemporary historians who place the site, generally on a small island, anywhere from Charlotte Harbor in the north to the area off the Everglades below Cape Romano in the south. Selection of these sites indicates a lack of knowledge of marine geography and probably stems to a large degree from use (or misuse) of Juan Lopez de Velasco's *Geographia de las Indias*, published in 1575.

Velasco was a landsman, not a seaman, and compiled his description of the west coast of Florida from a study of old charts and rutters. They either contained erroneous information or Velasco was unable to interpret them properly. He placed the Bay of Tocobaga (Tampa Bay) at 29½ degrees which is about 120 miles too far north. From that point south to the Bay of Carlos his distances and description of the shoreline make absolutely no sense when related to the actual bays, inlets, and rivers which he was attempting to describe. Yet this inaccurate and fallacious document has been used by misinformed historians when far better material on marine geography is available to determine the site of the Bay of Carlos and the island and village of Carlos.

My selection of Estero Island in San Carlos Bay is based not only upon the description of the area by Ponce de León and others who visited the area, but is pinned down quite definitely in the coastal survey ordered by Governor Fernandez de Olivera in 1612. Olivera sent ensign Juan Rodriguez de Cortaya, an experienced naval officer and navigator, with thirty soldiers in a launch to survey the coast from the Bay of Tocobaga (Tampa Bay) south to the Bay of Carlos.

Cortaya established the latitude of Tampa Bay at 27½ degrees, the latitude of Charlotte Harbor at 26⅙ degrees, and the island village of Carlos in the Bay of Carlos at 26 degrees. The reported latitudes of Tampa Bay and Charlotte Harbor are within one or two miles of their actual latitudes. Placement of the village on an island in the Bay of Carlos 1/6 degree (or ten nautical miles) south of Charlotte Harbor would fix it quite firmly on Estero Island in San Carlos Bay.

Cortaya described the village of Carlos as located on an island "within a large river and bar," which fits the geographical features of Estero Island in the mouth of the Caloosahatchee River perfectly. Although he didn't give the size of the island, he did state that he was met by more than sixty canoes and that Carlos was in a large canoe with forty people. This fact together with Fray Lopez's estimate of 400 for the population of the island would fit the size of Estero Island and not the size of the much smaller islands proposed by other historians. It is apparent from archaeological finds on the small Mound Key between Estero Island and the mainland that it served as a religious ceremonial site and burial ground for the main village on the island.

During the final fifty years of Calusa existence as a separate culture and society they clung steadfastly to their religion. They refused even to death to submit to the European opportunists who arrived after the demise of Spanish rule in Florida. The indomitable spirit of the Calusa Indians and their leaders is clearly the reason for the failure of Ponce de León and later Spaniards to make peace with them and found a colony in Florida. Those historians who say that it was Ponce de León's mistreatment of the Indians which caused his troubles and subsequently his death are quite wrong. The real reason is that Ponce de León unwittingly and through no fault of his own chose to found his colony in the territory of the intractable and unconquerable Calusa.

This ends the story of the failed Spanish colonization attempts in southwest Florida, beginning with Ponce de León's initial landing in 1513, and followed by his valiant but unsuccessful attempt to found a colony in 1521. One cannot help but reflect upon the fact that if only Ponce de León had been met by peaceful and passive Indians like those Menéndez found at St. Augustine instead of the bellicose and unfriendly Calusa, then Sanibel and probably Fort Myers could lay claim to being the oldest cities in the United States, preceding St. Augustine by many years.

In meeting his untimely death at the hands of the Calusa, Ponce de León was at least spared the unkind knowledge that later historians would pervert his courageous and enterprising exploration voyage into a vain and egocentric hunt for a fountain of youth. The time has come to cleanse our history books of this gross error and restore the significant voyage of Juan Ponce de León to its legitimate and true place in the history of early Spanish exploration.

Epilogue

"THE TIME HAS COME TO CLEANSE OUR HISTORY BOOKS OF THIS GROSS ERROR AND RESTORE THE SIGNIFICANT VOYAGE OF JUAN PONCE DE LEÓN TO ITS LEGITIMATE AND TRUE PLACE IN THE HISTORY OF EARLY SPANISH EXPLORATION."

This is one of those high sounding pronouncements which looks good in print but how does it stand up to the hard cold facts of reality? That's really quite a formidable task I have proposed, involving the expensive revision and reprinting of hundreds of thousands of history textbooks and encyclopedias.

Will it be done solely on the merits of this book? Of course not!

It will take far more than this modest effort by a navigator turned historian to bring about a change in long-held beliefs. I feel that my effort has not been in vain as I have brought the historical truths of the life and voyages of Juan Ponce de Léon to the readers of this narrative.

Juan Ponce de León has suffered through nearly five centuries from what we would call a "bad press." I have given to the reader the true story of this courageous Spanish explorer to clarify and correct the misinformation in our current history books. In this regard if I have just succeeded in getting my foot in the door, just to hold it open long enough for the light to shine through, then I feel we are well on the way to restoring "the significant voyage of Juan Ponce de León to its legitimate and true place in the history of early Spanish exploration."

Figure 22. Statue of Juan Ponce de León, erected 1923, in St. Augustine, Florida.

Bibliography

Arnade, Charles W. "Who Was Juan Ponce de León?" *Tequesta, The Journal of the Historical Association of Southern Florida,* XXVII (1967), 29–58.

Ballesteros Gabrois, Manuel. *La idea colonial de Ponce de Leon.* San Juan, Puerto Rico, 1960.

Boucher, Philip P. *Cannibal Encounters: Europeans and Island Caribs, 1492–1763.* Baltimore: The John Hopkins University Press, 1992.

Boucher, Philip P. "The Island Caribs: Present State of the Debate," *Terrae Incognitae, The Journal for the History of Discoveries,* XXIV (1992), 55–64.

Burland, C. A. *Peoples of the Sun.* New York and London: Praeger Publishers, Inc., 1976.

Chapelle, Howard I. *The History of American Sailing Ships.* New York: W. W. Norton & Company, 1965.

Cohen, J. M. *The Four Voyages of Christopher Columbus, from the biography of Columbus by his son Ferdinand.* London: Cresset Library, 1969.

Davis, T. Frederick. "History of Juan Ponce de León's Voyages to Florida: Source Records." *The Florida Historical Quarterly,* 14: 1 (1935), 1–49.

Dunn, Oliver C. and James E. Kelley, Jr. *The Diario of Christopher Columbus's First Voyage to America 1492–1493.* Norman: University of Oklahoma Press, 1989.

Gannon, Michael V. *The Cross in the Sand. The Early Catholic Church in Florida.* Gainesville: University of Florida Press, 1965.

Goldstein, Herman H. *New and Full Moons 1001 B.C. to A.D. 1651.* Philadelphia: American Philosophical Society, 1973.

Hanke, Lewis. *Aristotle and the American Indians.* Bloomington: Indiana University Press, 1959.

Hann, John H., ed. *Missions to the Calusa.* Gainesville: University of Florida Press, 1991.

Herrera, Antonio de. *Historia General de los Hechos de los Castellanos en las Islas i Tierra Firme del Mar Oceano.* Madrid, 1601–1615.

Jane, Cecil. *The Journal of Christopher Columbus.* (Edited and revised by L. A. Vigneras.) New York: Bramhall House, 1960.

Judge, Joseph. "Where Columbus Found the New World," *National Geographic Magazine,* 170: 5 (November 1986), 566–599.

Keegan, William F. "The Development and Extinction of Lucayan Society," *Terrae Incognitae, The Journal for the History of Discoveries,* XXIV (1992), 43–53.

Kelley, James E., Jr. "The Map of the Bahamas Implied by Chaves' Derrotero," *Imago Mundi,* 42 (1989) 26–49.

Kelley, James E., Jr. "Juan Ponce de León's Discovery of Florida: Herrera's Narrative Revisited," *Revista de Historia de America,* III (1992) 31–65.

Kelley, James E., Jr. Postulated 1513 Magnetic Variation. Personal communications, 1990.

Las Casas, Bartolomé de. *History of the Indies.* (Translated by Andree Collard.) New York: Harper & Row, 1971.

Lawson, Edward W. *The Discovery of Florida and its discoverer, Juan Ponce de León.* St. Augustine: privately published, 1946.

Lawson, Edward W. (with Walter B. Fraser). *The First Landing Place of Juan Ponce de León on the North American Continent in the Year 1513.* St. Augustine: privately published, 1956.

Lunde, Paul. "Ponce de León and an Arab Legend," *Aramco World* 43: 3, (May/June, 1992), 43–46.

Lyon, Eugene. *The Enterprise of Florida: Pedro Menéndez de Aviles and the Spanish Conquest.* University Presses of Florida, 1965.

MacLeish, W. H. *The Gulf Stream.* New York: Houghton Mifflin Co., 1989.

Marden, Luis. "The First Landfall of Columbus," *National Geographic Magazine*, 170: 5 (November 1986), 572–577.

McIntosh, Gregory C. "Martin Alonzo Pinzón's Discovery of Babueca and the Identity of Guanahaní," *Terrae Incognitae, The Journal for the History of Discoveries,* XXIV (1992), 79–100.

Morison, Samuel Eliot. *The European Discovery of America: The Northern Voyages A.D. 500–1600.* New York: Oxford University Press, 1971.

Morison, Samuel Eliot. *The European Discovery of America: The Southern Voyages A.D. 1492–1616.* New York: Oxford University Press, 1974.

Murga Sanz, Vicente. *Juan Ponce de León: fundador y primer gobernador del pueblo puertorriqueno, descubridor de la Florida y del Estrecho de las Bahamas.* San Juan: University of Puerto Rico, 1959.

Olschki, Leonardo. "Ponce de León's Fountain of Youth: History of a Geographical Myth," *The Hispanic American Historical Review,* XXI: 3 (August 1941), 361–385.

Peck, Douglas T. "Reconstruction and Analysis of the 1513 Discovery Voyage of Juan Ponce de León," *The Florida Historical Quarterly,* LXXI: 2 (October 1992), 133–154.

Peck, Douglas T. "Gooney Bird Seeks Columbus Landfall Site," *South Florida History*, 20 (1992) 5–9.

Peck, Douglas T. *Why Did Ponce de León Fail to Find His Fabulous Island of Bimini?* Bradenton, Florida: privately published, 1990.

Prescott, William Hickling. *History of the Conquest of Mexico.* Philadelphia: J. B. Lippincott Company, 1873.

Prescott, William Hickling. *The Rise and Decline of the Spanish Empire.* New York: Dorset Press, 1990.

Robertson, James A., editor and translator. *True Relation of the Hardships Suffered by Governor Fernando de Soto and Certain Portuguese Gentlemen During the Discovery of the Province of Florida. Now Newly Set Forth by a Gentleman of Elvas.* Deland: The Florida State Historical Society, 1932–3, 2 vols.

Sanz, Eufemio Lorenzo. *Conquistadors of America.* Valladolid: 1984.

Schell, Rolfe F. *De Soto Did Not Land at Tampa Bay.* Ft. Myers Beach: Island Press, 1966.

Schott, C. A. *An Inquiry Into the Variation of the Compass at the Time of the landfall of Columbus in the Bahamas in 1492.* Washington, D. C.: U. S. Coast and Geodetic Survey, 1880.

Scisco, L. D. "The track of Ponce de León in 1513," *Bulletin of the American Geographical Society,* 45 (1913), 721–735.

Sealey, Neil. "Ponce de León's Voyage in 1513 Points to San Salvador As Landfall of Columbus In 1492," *Encounter* 92, 3: 3 (1989), 4–5.

Smith, Buckingham. See "True."

Swanson, John R. *Final Report of the U. S. De Soto Expedition Commission.* Washington, D. C.: U. S. Government Printing Office, 1939.

Taviani, Paolo Emilio. *Christopher Columbus—The Grand Design,* London: Orbis Publishing, 1985.

Tío, Aurelio. "Historia del Descubrimiento de la Florida y Bimeni o Yucatan," *Boletin de la Academia Puertorriquena de la Historia,* 2: 8 (1972), 7–267.

True, David O. "Some Early Maps Relating to Florida," *Imago Mundi,* XI (1954), 73–84.

True, David O., ed. *Memoir of D. d'Escalante Fontaneda, Respecting Florida.* (Translated by Buckingham Smith.) University of Miami and Historical Society of Southern Florida, 1944.

Weddle, Robert S. *Spanish Sea—The Gulf of Mexico in North American Discovery, 1500–1685.* Fort Worth: Texas A & M University Press, 1985.

Widmer, Randolph J. *The Evolution of the Calusa: A Nonagricultural Chiefdom on the Southwest Florida Coast.* Tuscaloosa and London: University of Alabama Press, 1988.

Wilkinson, Warren H. *Opening the Case Against the Final Report of the U. S. De Soto Expedition Commission.* Jacksonville, Florida, 1960.

List of Illustrations

Unless otherwise indicated, all illustrations are original drawings made by the author. Information as to the source of some illustrations is appropriately noted.

Index